The BHS

Training Manual

FOR

Progressive
Riding Tests 1-6

The BHS
Training Manual
FOR
Progressive
Riding Tests 1-6

THE BRITISH HORSE SOCIETY

Islay Auty FBHS

KENILWORTH PRESS

First published in 2003 by
Kenilworth Press Ltd
Addington
Buckingham
MK18 2JR

British Library Cataloguing in Publication Data
A catalogue record for this book is available from the British Library.

ISBN 0-872119-57-3

Layout by Kenilworth Press

Printed in Great Britain by MPG Books Ltd (www.mpg-books.co.uk)

DISCLAIMER: The authors and publishers shall have neither
liability nor responsibility to any person or entity with respect to
any loss or damage caused or alleged to be caused directly or
indirectly by the information contained in this book. While the
book is as accurate as the authors can make it, there may be errors,
omissions, and inaccuracies.

Contents

Picture acknowledgements

All line drawings are by **Dianne Breeze**, with the exception of those on pages 74 (right), and 100, which are by **Carole Vincer**.

The arena diagrams on pages 44, 45 and 64 are by **Michael J. Stevens**.

Picture sources
The author and publishers wish to acknowledge the following books as sources for some of the illustrations:

- **The BHS Manual of Equitation**, Consultant Editor Islay Auty FBHS, published by Kenilworth Press

- **The BHS Complete Manual of Stable Management**, Consultant Editor Islay Auty FBHS, published by Kenilworth Press

- **Threshold Picture Guide No. 8, Field Management**, by Mary Gordon Watson, published by Kenilworth Press

- **Threshold Picture Guide No. 16, Feet and Shoes**, by Toni Webber, published by Kenilworth Press

- **The Horsemaster's Notebook**, by Mary Rose, published by Kenilworth Press

- **Teaching Children to Ride**, by Jane Wallace, published by Kenilworth Press

Introduction

What are Progressive Riding Tests?

Progressive Riding Tests are proficiency tests offered by British Horse Society Approved riding establishments. They are intended for any clients who are interested in working towards a certificate which demonstrates their competence at various levels in riding and stable management. There are six tests, ranging from 1, at the lowest level, to 6, at the highest.

Each test is divided into riding (equitation) and stable management, so that the subjects can be studied separately. For example, a non-rider may be interested solely in the care of the horse; alternatively, a competent rider may not yet possess the practical skills required for the same level of stable management.

It is likely that you first heard about Progressive Riding Tests from your BHS riding school. Many centres use the tests to motivate riders to improve, which in turn develops self-esteem and further enthusiasm for future study.

How are they accessed?

Any British Horse Society Approved riding establishment can offer Progressive Riding Tests (PRTs) at its centre. How courses are run is entirely left to each individual centre. The tests may be incorporated into the school's normal riding lessons, at different levels of competence; other schools run lessons or courses specifically designed around the tests. Some centres charge an 'all-in' rate for training and examining, which includes the syllabus card and certificate (when achieved); others make separate charges for training, examining and paperwork. Usually the school obtains all the necessary information from the BHS Riding Schools Office. This will include syllabi, test cards and certificates. The centre organises the training and ultimately the testing or examining of each level. The 'examiner' will be a BHS-Registered Instructor, possibly your regular instructor. For tests level 1 to 4, the 'examiner' must be a minimum of BHSAI. For tests level 5 and 6, the registered instructor (examiner) must be at least a BHSII. Again there is no stipulation for the 'examiner' to be an outside person;

it is perfectly acceptable for the instructor to be 'in house'.

Training and examining

As already stated, the method of training and examining is entirely at the discretion of each individual establishment. In future chapters, in which the various tests are looked at in detail, you will see that each test is clearly split up into elements. This enables the school to work on one or two elements at a time until a person is competent, before moving on to the next element(s). It also allows the school the choice of examining a test as a whole, or of letting people attain elements of the test and gradually build up to completing the test piecemeal, without the 'stress' of an exam on the whole content in one go.

Don't worry if your riding school does not employ an instructor above BHSAI level. As you progress to Tests 5 and 6 your school will arrange for an instructor of BHSII level or above to visit and take you through the higher levels.

The length of training depends on many factors, some of which may be listed as follows:

- How often you ride (once a week, more or less).

- How intense the training is for a specific test. (If your riding is in a standard class lesson your progress may be a little slower than if your instructor is working specifically on the test requirements with the whole group.)

- How hard you work and how strongly you commit yourself to learning, both in the riding and the practical stable management.

- The centre may set a timescale to help schedule the training for a specific level of test. Each week a new aspect of the syllabus may be worked on, with emphasis on repetition to consolidate competence.

- How much time and money you are able to spend on it.

Being examined or tested for anything, often induces a degree of apprehension in the candidate. Even if you know your instructor (examiner), being in an examiner–candidate situation inevitably gives you some heightened anxiety or nerves. It is the examiner's job to put you at ease as much as possible. However, it is your responsibility to leave those initial nerves behind you – once you commence your required tasks, you should concentrate on giving your best and try not to worry about what you might not know or be able to do.

It is the centre's responsibility to source the examiner, if he or she is not 'in house', and arrange payment as appropriate. This cost may be accounted for in the charge made by the centre, to train for and take the Progressive Riding Tests.

The link between Progressive Riding Tests and Stage 1

The Progressive Riding Tests, as described, are simple tests of proficiency at various levels. They are designed to be implemented by your BHS Approved riding school to give you something to work towards as your skills in riding, handling and caring for the horse develop. They can be worked through as slowly or as quickly as you choose, or as your riding skill dictates. As you will see in the ensuing text, the tests increase in demands, both in riding and ability to care for the horse, from Test 1 through to Test 6. At Test 6 level, if you compare the demands of the test (e.g. the riding) with the requirements of the BHS Stage 1 Riding section, you will see that the degree of competence required for both is very similar. In fact the ridden section of Progressive Riding Test 6 requires the rider to be able to canter without stirrups, which is not a requirement of Stage 1 – which means that the rider who has progressed to PRT 6 is technically a little more competent than the Stage 1 rider.

There is a link between PRTs 1–6 and BHS Stage 1. If you choose to continue to study and progress your level of competence above PRT 6 then the natural pathway would be to consider taking BHS Stage exams.

As we will see, the competence of PRTs 1–6 accumulates to give a similar status of ability to a holder of BHS Stage 1. Therefore if you achieve Progressive Riding Tests 1–6 and you wish then to follow on with BHS Stage exams, you have exemption from taking BHS Stage 1 and can progress directly to Stage 2. On production of the relevant certificates for PRTs 1–6 to the BHS Examinations Office (see address at the back of the book) you will be given an exemption for Stage 1 and will be able to make an application directly to take Stage 2 when your ability allows.

When to use the link

Let's assume you have learned to ride in a BHS Approved establishment. You are really 'bitten by the horse bug' but not able to have a horse of your own. Ask your riding school about the Progressive Riding Tests, obtain a copy of the test syllabi from your riding school. Ask your school or instructor whether you can study for the tests. This may already be done in the school. If the tests are not used, there is no reason why you should not still be able to work towards the levels in your weekly lessons. The chapters which break down the work in each test should help you to focus on what you need to know and how you go about obtaining the knowledge and practical competence.

Hopefully the riding school will have a system in place to work their clients towards achieving the PRTs. If they don't, ask them to implement one.

You work on steadily to achieve all six tests and wonder what you can do next? This would be the time when you might join an evening class or a group working towards BHS Stages, and your next aim could be Stage 2 having obtained your exemption on Stage 1.

Many children who learn to ride in a riding school and then become very keen 'weekend helpers', progress in their mid teens to become very committed to 'working with horses'. If these young people have taken PRTs in their riding school then this can be very useful when they choose to go into horses as a full-time career. By achieving PRTs 1–6, again they would be able to access Stage 2 directly, which would save the exam fee for Stage 1. The Progressive Riding Tests inevitably have a cost attached to them, but often the fees are spread over months or more, and this is much easier to absorb than a lump sum for an exam fee.

Why choose Progressive Riding Tests?

Progressive Riding Tests would probably be a good choice:

- If you want to make each step quite simple and undemanding – each PRT has clear criteria of competence which can be achieved relatively easily within the progress of weekly riding lessons.

- If you want a small investment of time and/or money which could be more or less in line with the weekly lesson.

- If you want to aim for riding and stable management separately.

- If you are not interested in anything other than simple bench-marks of your competence as it develops.

- If your riding school offers good groups or classes working towards PRTs and you enjoy the camaraderie of like-minded people working for the same goal.

Note that you do not need to be a member of the BHS to take PRTs; however, they are run **only** at BHS Approved riding establishments.

Progressive Riding
Tests 1–6

For each of the six tests:

- We will discuss each element of both the stable management and the riding.

- We will define what the examiner would be looking for in a competent person.

- We will consider how and where that competence can be achieved by the candidate.

IMPORTANT: Candidates are advised to check that they are working from the latest test syllabus, as test content and procedure are liable to alteration. Contact the BHS Riding Schools/Approvals Department for up-to-date information regarding the syllabus.

Progressive Riding Test 1

STABLE MANAGEMENT

Approach a horse/pony safely

From your first experience of a horse in your first riding lesson, you should have been taught about the need for awareness and safety around the animal. By the nature of its size alone, if a horse stands on you it is likely to hurt and may injure you. It is essential that you are always 'aware' when around the horse. Make sure that the horse always knows where you are, can see you and knows when you are likely to touch or handle him. You can improve your safety awareness by handling horses regularly and with a feeling for wanting to understand what makes them 'tick'.

The examiner would look for:

- Confidence and a quiet, positive approach to the horse.

- Good awareness of yourself in relation to the horse, the horse knowing you are there.

Put on a headcollar

Make sure your instructor has shown you a safe and practical procedure for placing the horse's nose into the headcollar, passing the strap over his head, behind his ears, and fastening the strap on the nearside.

The examiner would look for:

- Quiet but confident handling of the horse.

- Proficient handling of the headcollar, placing it on and attaching it with maximum efficiency and minimum inconvenience to the horse.

Tie up a horse/pony

Make sure that your instructor has shown you how to tie a quick-release knot, which should always be used for tying up a horse, so that in an emergency he can be quickly released. It is always advisable to tie the rope to a loop of string rather than directly to a metal tie-ring. Then in the event of the horse pulling back, the string will break and not the headcollar (which would be much more costly). Practise a quick-release knot frequently until it is automatic to you.

The examiner would look for:

- A horse tied with a quick-release knot, the lead rope passed through a loop of string instead of directly tied to a tie-ring.

- The horse tied quickly and efficiently.

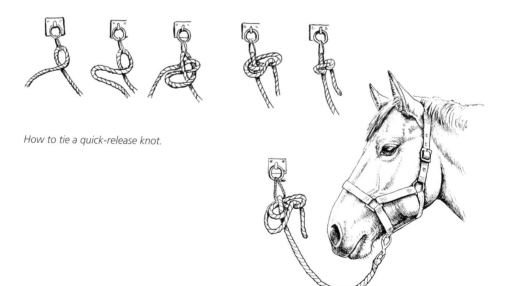

How to tie a quick-release knot.

Lead a horse/pony

Leading a horse or pony takes practice. The horse must walk quietly and obediently with his head in front of you, while you are approximately level with his neck or withers. The rein should be held in both hands but with relaxation and alertness. You must be capable of leading with authority so that the horse walks

How not to lead a horse/pony.

How not to lead a horse/pony. Don't turn to face the horse and pull.

The correct way to lead a horse/pony.

When turning, turn the horse away from you.

or trots obediently by your side. When you turn a horse while leading, always turn him away from you. This is much safer as it keeps control of the horse's hindquarters and prevents him from swinging them out.

The examiner would look for:

- Confidence in you; purposeful walking or running so that the horse takes his lead from you.

- Both hands firmly on the rein, but keeping the horse's head relaxed (i.e. hands not holding too tightly).

- Turning the horse away from you correctly.

Hold a quiet horse/pony for inspection, shoeing or clipping

You must be able to hold a sensible horse while he is being shod or clipped. This requires you to be responsible for him standing still and not getting fractious. You must be able to be firm but soothing or reassuring to encourage him to

How to stand a horse up for inspection.

stand quietly. For inspection it is preferable to encourage the horse to stand on all four feet evenly and stand up as square as possible.

The examiner would look for:

- You being able to control the horse and make him stand still and as balanced (on all four feet) as possible.

- You being quietly confident and reassuring to the horse.

General behaviour points about the horse/pony in the stable

This knowledge will only come with gradual experience of seeing and dealing with horses in stables. You should develop an understanding of how the horse demonstrates contentment, anxiety, fear, aggression, reluctance, and so on. You should be able to recognise when a horse looks hungry, tired, cold or hot. You should know when the horse is eating and drinking normally and when his body functions are normal.

The examiner would question this area. For example:

- What signs tell you the horse is content? Nervous? Frightened?

- What points of behaviour in the stable would tell you that all was well?

Know different colours of horses

You can accrue this information through your own reading and research. Ask other people about the coat colour of every horse you ever see. Read books and magazine articles about colours and breeds of horses.

The examiner would look for:

- A basic knowledge of most of the common colours of horses.

- If there are a limited number of horses to use for practical purposes of identifying colour, then you may be asked to describe a 'bay', a 'roan', or some other colour.

Know signs of good health

This can be learned theoretically, which can help you to remember each point – e.g. shiny coat, bright eye, alertness to surroundings – but you must apply it practically as well. Look at different horses to learn to recognise different behaviour traits and signs of good health. Ask your instructor to tell you if there is a horse in the yard who is off colour for any reason and then go and look at him so that you recognise the horse that is not in good health.

The examiner would look for:

- You must know the various signs of a horse in good health and be able to list them, but you must also be able to apply the points that you have learned to the living horse in front of you.

Know various points of the horse

These can all be learned from a good horse book, but you **MUST** then apply them to a real horse so that you can identify them in the flesh.

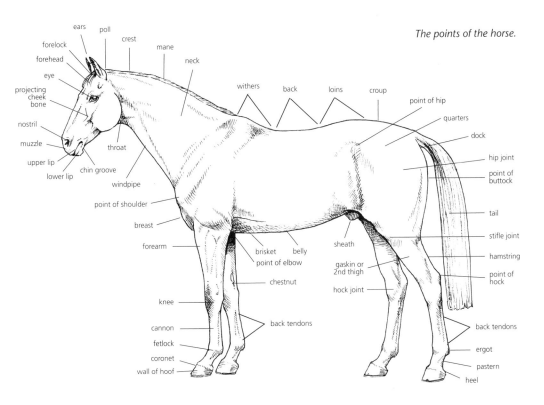

The points of the horse.

The examiner would probably ask you to identify :

- Any points of the horse, but will often pick on things like the hock/fetlock/ withers/poll/pastern/gaskin.

Know how to correctly pick out the horse's feet

You must ask your instructor to show you how to pick out the feet and then you must practise it **OFTEN**. There is a knack to learning how to encourage the horse to pick up each of his feet; it is easier to pick out all four from the same side. You should be aware of the safe way to handle the hind leg, and the correct way to use the hoof pick in a downward way from heel to toe.

The examiner will look for:

- Competent and confident handling of the horse and efficiency in getting the horse to pick up his feet.

How to pick up a near fore.

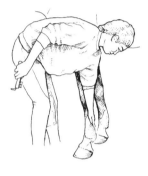

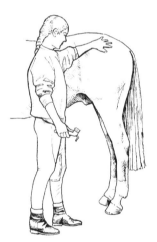

How to pick up a near hind.

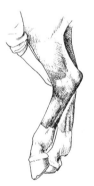

Safe handling of the off hind from the near side.

- Safe handling of the hind legs.

- Competent use of the hoof pick.

Know how to turn out to grass and how to catch up

This is a task that you must do regularly, with supervision and guidance from your instructor to begin with. Learning to catch a horse is an amalgamation of approaching confidently and safely, fitting the headcollar, leading in and tying up, and then the reverse to turn the horse out again.

Awareness of other horses is imperative, both in bringing one horse in and leaving others out, or bringing in a number of horses (requiring several of you to manage), and similarly in turning them back out again. There are a number of safety implications including the management of the gate, turning horses out safely so that no one risks being kicked.

The following points must be considered and would be looked for or asked for by an examiner:

To turn out

- Consider how many horses are to be turned out. Ideally, one person per horse.

- One competent person to manage the gate.

- All horses to be led well into the field, the gate closed, and all horses in a space away from each other, turned back to face the gate.

- All horses released at the same time (one person to advise when).

To catch the horse(s)

- Prepare by having one person per horse (ideally) and a headcollar for each horse.

- One person to control the gate.

- Make a quiet approach to the horse, letting him know where you are.

- Approach from the front and slightly to the side.

- Competent fitting and securing of the headcollar.

- Leading in firmly and keeping space between horses.

Know the correct, safe clothing to wear in and around the yard and when handling horses

This should have been explained to you on your first visit to the yard, and will have subsequently been demonstrated to you by everyone involved in the establishment where you ride. You should have already adopted a clothing code in keeping with the policy of the yard.

The examiner would expect to see:

- Safe footwear (no soft shoes or trainers).

- Always a riding hat when mounted.

- Gloves for added safety when leading horses.

- No dangling ear-rings or jewellery which might become caught.

- No fashion-type clothing or perfume.

- Practical, close-fitting, warm and waterproof clothing as weather dictates.

PRT1 EQUITATION

Be able to maintain a correct, balanced position at walk and trot

You must be able to show a good basic position which is independent of the reins in walk and trot. By working hard in your lessons to develop basic security in the saddle, with your hands co-ordinated and not relying on the reins for balance or support, you will become more effective in your position and influence on the horse.

Work without stirrups is essential to help further your depth of seat. Concentrate on your own suppleness and relaxation as this will also improve your balance and feel for the horse.

Developing a good basic position is one of the foundation stones for all your subsequent riding.

The examiner would look for:

- A balanced position, showing weight taken evenly on both seat bones, with a straight line from the ear to the shoulder, through the hip to the heel, with another straight line from the elbow, through the wrist and rein to the horse's mouth.

The correct position for the rider, as seen from the side. Notice the shoulder–hip–heel alignment.

- Relaxation and suppleness in your position.

- Confidence in your ability to adjust your balance, if at any time you lose it, and to quickly re-establish a good basic position.

- Your position being sustained throughout the work period, not starting well and gradually deteriorating.

Mount and dismount, being assisted (leg-up) or from a mounting block

Mounting is something that you should learn in your very first riding lesson and then work to perfect in the interests of the horse's comfort and well-being. Poor mounting will not only compromise your safety, but also will compromise the horse's comfort. Good mounting will ultimately ensure your safety, which is of paramount importance. Practise and practise, until you are competent and as agile as possible. Learning to give or receive a leg-up is a skill which you must take time to develop. Encourage someone who is good at leg-ups to show you the technique. It is the timing of the spring up (from the rider) and the 'push' from the person giving the leg-up that dictates the success of a good leg-up. It has nothing to do with strength. A good leg-up, given and received, is a light and co-ordinated movement between giver and receiver. Just watch jockeys being legged-up in the paddock at a race meeting.

The examiner is looking for:

- Control of the horse while mounting and an energetic active mounting procedure.

- Control of the rider's weight onto the horse's back as he or she mounts.

- Co-ordination between giver and receiver of the leg-up.

- A light and agile movement from the rider, and light, controlled lowering of the seat onto the horse's back.

- Control of the horse throughout any method of mounting.

Mounting from the ground.

reins short enough to control
horse and prevent him moving off;
right hand holds the stirrup

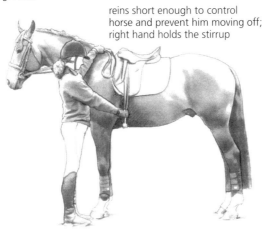

right hand must go well over
to the offside of the saddle

avoid digging left
toe into horse's
ribs, which could
upset him

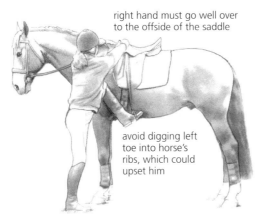

right leg must clear the
horse's quarters athletically;
weight must be lowered, with
control, lightly into the saddle

Correct leading of the horse/pony with a bridle

This activity should be completely familiar to you if you have routinely led your horse/pony from the stable to the riding school or arena prior to mounting. Always lead with the reins over the head (unless the horse is wearing a standing martingale, in which case leave the reins over the neck). Lead the horse on the nearside and demonstrate authority and control in the same way as leading the horse in hand in a headcollar. If the horse is wearing a bridle, it gives you a little more control if anything unexpected happens. Practise leading in hand with a bridle. In turning the horse, always remember to turn the horse away from you.

Leading the horse, with a bridle.

Leading a horse, with a bridle and martingale.

The examiner will look for:

- Firmness and authority with the horse, but sympathetic handling and empathy.

- Good positioning (just in front of the horse's shoulder) to be able to influence the horse under all circumstances.

- The reins short enough to be in control but not so tense as to make the horse anxious and uncertain because you are nervous.

- Ability to walk and trot (if conditions and surroundings permit) and correctly turn the horse around and return.

Checking of girth and stirrups on and off the horse/pony whilst stationary

This should be a task or tasks that you have been involved with from your earliest riding lessons, albeit with assistance in the early stages. Always check girths and run down stirrups before mounting. After a few minutes of riding in then you should look to 'check the girth'. More able riders can check it themselves, but if in doubt then the instructor should help the less able members of the ride to adjust girths and stirrups safely. Practise making the stirrups comfortable when in the saddle.

The examiner will look for:

- A length of stirrup leather that will allow you to adopt as good a position as possible.

- Your ability to feel if your stirrups are not level. This is a priority. If there are mirrors in the school, then use them, particularly when you are riding straight towards them.

- Your ability to check stirrup length and girths on you own, albeit at halt first, and then later, if necessary, on the move as well.

Walk and trot

You will have worked a great deal in your lessons in walk and trot. You should be striving to sustain a good quality rhythm in whatever pace you are riding.

Continue to develop your position in walk and trot and through the transitions from one pace to another. Continue to develop greater depth through your commitment to your position and therefore improve your balance, co-ordination and effect every time you ride.

The examiner will look for:

- Balance and position in walk and trot.

- Your ability to move in balance from one gait to another and not interfere with the horse.

- Your awareness of your own balance and effect in walk and trot. The horse is a living, breathing, feeling, animal and the rider ignores this at his or her peril.

- Your ability to be able to ride around the school in walk and/or trot.

Know the aids to make the horse/pony walk

Aids for changing pace should be a familiar part of your riding. You must feel completely at ease with recalling and then describing the aids for walk. Practise vocalising the aids in the following order:

- Inside leg (inside to the direction of the bend) 'on the girth' sends the horse forward.

- Outside leg (a little behind the girth) supports the forward movement and controls the quarters.

- Inside rein creates the slight flexion in the direction of movement through turns and circles.

- Outside rein controls the degree of bend and regulates the pace.

The examiner may ask:

- You to describe the aids for walking.

- May want to see you demonstrate the ability to make the horse walk.

Know the aids to make the horse/pony halt

You must be confident to describe and able to apply the aids for halt. This should be something that is familiar to you through practice in your weekly lessons.

The examiner will want to see:

- You make smooth, well-prepared transitions to halt from walk.

Know the aids to make the horse/pony trot

These aids should also be familiar to you through your weekly lessons. Make sure that you can describe the aids easily, even when you are feeling nervous or apprehensive.

The examiner will want to see:

- You demonstrate the ability to make the horse/pony trot.

- You describe the aids you used to make the change of pace.

Know the correct standard of riding hat and how to adjust it properly

The riding hat should carry a BSI kite mark and number to designate the level of protection offered. When you purchased your first hat (ideally from a reputable

Correctly fitted crash cap with silk. Hair neatly tucked away.

Hat too large and perched on the back of the head giving no protection to the forehead.

If the chinstrap is too loose, the hat can slip back and become dislodged.

saddlery outfitters) you should have been given advice an appropriate hats and on fitting, from a member of staff. Riding instructors are not 'qualified' to give formal advice about hats, other than that mounted riders should always wear them.

The examiner will ensure:

- That every candidate owns his or her own hat and that the hat sits correctly on the rider's head and will ultimately offer some protection.

- That you have some understanding of the importance of hats as a rider.

- That the chin strap is always fastened when riding.

Note: Candidates may complete the stable management element separately from the equitation section. Both sections must be achieved to give the Progressive Riding Test 1 certificate.

Progressive Riding Test 2

STABLE MANAGEMENT

Know the parts of a saddle and snaffle bridle

If you are riding weekly, then it is hoped that you will be handling your horse a little, even if only to lead him out to mount. You will lead him out by the bridle and ride on the saddle. From an interest point of view you should already know the basic parts of the tack. You can either enhance that knowledge from a book (such as *The BHS Complete Manual of Stable Management*) or you can ask your instructor to name all the parts of the equipment. Then you must learn them by heart.

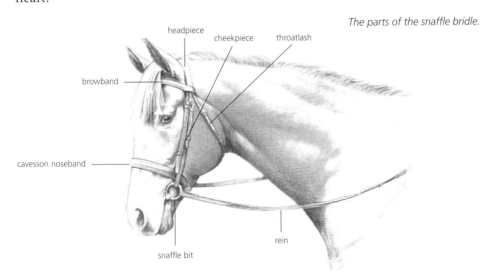

The parts of the snaffle bridle.

headpiece
cheekpiece
throatlash
browband
cavesson noseband
rein
snaffle bit

The parts of the saddle.

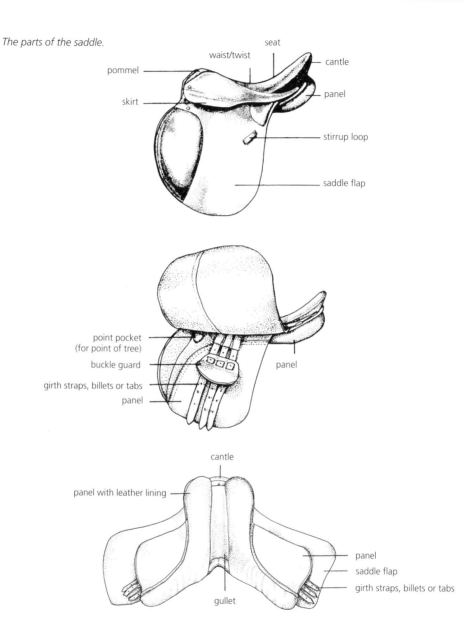

The examiner will look for:

- Your ability to name the various parts of the snaffle bridle and saddle, and probably to identify these parts on the tack itself.

Demonstrate how to clean the saddle and bridle

It is almost certain that at some stage you will have seen saddlery being cared for in the riding school. This would include regular cleaning by 'washing', to remove grease and dirt, and then application of saddle soap to maintain the tack in supple condition.

The actual system for cleaning tack is best learned from a practical demonstration, but this may follow easily from reading about the theory in a book. Thereafter practise cleaning tack until you become proficient. Cleaning tack should be a very satisfying activity.

The examiner will look for:

- A well-practised procedure which demonstrates competence.

- Effective cleaning and soaping of the leather, without an unnecessary amount of water being used which may dry out the tack.

Recognise tack that is in good and poor order

Ideally all tack should be maintained in good order in the interests of the safety and welfare of both horse and rider. You should be able to recognise the difference between supple, well-cared-for leather, and leather which has been neglected. The latter will dry out and eventually crack. Tack which is not looked after will soon cause discomfort or injury to horse and/or rider. Look around the tack room in the yard and see if you can find tack that is no longer in use. The chances are that it may have been left to dry out and deteriorate.

Read about or discuss with your instructor what tack in poor condition looks like.

The examiner will expect:

- You to be able to recognise the difference between tack that is well looked after and tack that is not cared for.

- You to describe what tack in poor condition may look like if there are no examples in your yard.

Care of the horse/pony after removing saddlery

How you look after the horse/pony when the tack is removed depends on whether he is hot and sweaty, and also on the weather conditions. The priority is always the welfare of the horse/pony. Wearing tack must not inconvenience him. Brushing or washing the area where the tack has made contact with the horse will be appropriate. You should learn from your instructor which action is required when – for example, it would be unusual to wash off the horse in very cold weather.

The examiner will expect you to:

- Know when to brush off the horse when the tack is removed.

- When washing might be more appropriate.

- Perhaps demonstrate what to do when the tack is removed.

Demonstrate how to skip out and set-fair a bed

This procedure applies to the management of the horse's bed during the day, to maintain it in a tidy, comfortable and presentable state.

You should first learn how to remove the droppings (skip out) when the stable is empty. Then, when you can skip out and make the bed tidy (lay the bedding flat and arrange a small amount of bedding around the walls of the stable) in an empty stable, you can learn to do it with a horse resident. Always remember that when working in the stable the horse must be tied up safely. Practising these tasks will give you competence and give you more confidence in carrying out the job.

The examiner will look for:

- A basic familiarity with handling the tools (skip, shovel or fork and broom and perhaps wheelbarrow).

- Safe management of the tools so that they do not inconvenience either yourself or the horse.

- The ability to skip out and set-fair the bed in a reasonably practical timescale.

(Taking an hour to complete it perfectly would not demonstrate practical competence. Around 5 to 15 minutes would be acceptable.)

- Completing the job without unnecessary waste of time or bedding.

Demonstrate how to muck out a bed

Nowhere is it possible to enjoy horses in stables without the necessity of 'mucking out'. Mucking out is traditionally recognised as being part of the practical
'hands on' commitment to horse ownership. Mucking out a full bed (shavings,
straw or any of the other types of bedding available e.g. paper) requires removal
of the soiled bedding (droppings and wet), sweeping the floor and replacement
of clean bedding. Ask your instructor to show you the procedure for mucking
out a stable well. Any book will tell you how to do it, but there is no substitute
for a practical demonstration. Then you need to practise. As with setting fair,
the task requires a reasonable timescale of completion to confer competence.
Once proficient, you should be able to muck out the average stable (12ft x 12ft/
4m x 4m) fully in 10 to 20 minutes.

The examiner will look for:

- A systematic approach to the task (for example, collect tools, remove droppings,
  stack clean bedding, remove wet areas, sweep floor, re-lay bedding).

- Safe management of the horse if he is still in the stable (i.e. tied up).

- The task completed competently in a reasonable period of time.

Know how to build and maintain a muck heap

A well-maintained and tidy muck heap nearly always reflects the overall standards of the yard. It is the responsibility of everyone involved in the yard to 'do
their bit'. Regular throwing up of the muck and then levelling off the heap will
maintain it in a tidy format. Learn the technique from someone with more
experience; ask them to show you how to throw up the muck and then system-
atically build it up in steps and levels.

The examiner may:

- Question you about how to look after the muck heap and why it is important.

- Take you to look at and discuss the yard's muck heap.

Knowledge of the grooming equipment and the importance of cleanliness

You may already be involved in 'brushing off' the horse before you ride. Learning more fully about grooming can give you much to work on, in the theoretical understanding about why horses need grooming, what equipment to use under different circumstances and how to use it. Having studied the theory of grooming, watch competent people grooming horses well. Ask your instructor to show you how to groom competently and then to supervise your procedure to make sure that you do it well. Grooming is a very important aspect of horse care.

The examiner will look for:

- A clear understanding of the reasons for grooming.

- An ability to name most of the most common items of grooming equipment, and knowledge about when and how they might be used.

- Reasons for the importance of cleanliness.

Know and be able to demonstrate the correct grooming procedure

This easily carries on from the last requirement. Naturally once you have learned the terms for all the tools and you have watched someone competent grooming, you should want to practise it yourself. Only practice will engender competence. Grooming should be a very rewarding activity for you and the horse.

The examiner will look for:

- A clear understanding of which piece of equipment you use for what part of the grooming and why.

- Practical competence in using the various brushes effectively so that the horse is cleaned and well groomed.

- Safe but practical handling of the horse while grooming.

- An easy and confident manner around the horse when working with him and grooming him.

Care of the mane and tail

The mane and tail require specialist treatment, because the hair is permanent (it continues growing throughout life, whereas the rest of the coat – except the fetlock hair – sheds twice a year). You must show a clear understanding of how to manage the mane and, quite separately, the tail.

The examiner will:

- Certainly expect you to know how to manage carefully the delicate hairs of the tail.

- Perhaps ask you to demonstrate how you would brush the mane and 'finger' the tail, avoiding using a brush on the tail.

- Expect you to know how often and when the tail (and or mane) would be washed.

Rules of watering

Water is the most important commodity for the continued well-being of the horse. You should read up on the rules for watering and then encourage your instructor to show you how those rules are incorporated into the day-to-day running of your riding school. The horse could not survive for long without water (three to four days), although he could exist for much longer without food (three to four weeks).

The examiner would expect you to know:

- That an average horse (stabled) might expect to use four (2 gallon/9 litre) buckets per day (8 gallons/36 litres). Obviously weather conditions might affect that.

- That the horse should always be given clean, fresh water.

- That the horse should only be allowed small sips of water fairly frequently after strenuous exercise, and that ideally water should never be withheld under any circumstances – although the amount of water taken in may be regulated in the horse's interest (e.g. immediately after hard or fast work).

- That the horse should always have water (or water accessible) prior to being fed. Large amounts of water consumed after a feed may wash the semi-digested food out of the stomach before more complete digestion has taken place.

Demonstrate how to carry a bucket of water correctly

Unless the yard has an automatic watering system available to the horses, then carrying water in buckets will be an integral part of the daily care of the horses. Carrying a bucket full of water requires a certain technique, one that will prevent you from spilling water down your leg or across the yard and prevents you from suffering any strain from carrying the weight of a full bucket. It is easier to carry two full buckets than one because the weight is then evenly balanced over both sides of your body. Watch someone competent carrying water and pay special attention to the way the buckets are picked up. The handler should have a straight back and bent knees so that there is minimal strain on the back. Practise this task well.

The examiner will look for:

- Your ability to pick up one or two buckets correctly to minimise strain.

- Competent, practised handling of full bucket(s) so that the minimum amount, if any, is spilt.

How to pick up two buckets correctly.

Know how to lift a sack of feed

As with carrying water, the aim in carrying heavy feed sacks (20–25kg) is to minimise the risk of injury to your back. It is important to learn how to pick up the sack (knees bent, and carry the weight close to your body and supported on your chest – in front – or on your shoulder). Learn how to pick up and carry weight by watching someone who knows how to do this easily and fluently. Then practise, perhaps starting with smaller weights and building up to larger ones, particularly if you are a small person or not very strong.

The examiner will look for:

- Your technique for picking up the weight with- out risk of injury.

- Your ability to manage to carry a feed sack competently.

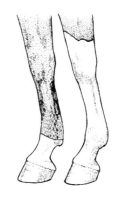

How to pick up a feed sack – knees bent, back straight, with the weight supported on the torso.

Know markings of the horse

As in recognising colours of horses, learning the markings of horses and the names for these different features should be an interesting task and is easily learned from a good book about horses. Identifying markings may be vital if you ever need to fill in a veterinary identification form for your horse or, in the worst case scenario, if you have to give identifying features of a horse because he has been stolen or lost. Ask your instructor or some other knowledgeable horse person about markings. Learn the difference between, for example, stockings and socks, blazes and snips.

Sock (left) and stocking markings.

HEAD MARKINGS

| Star | Star and stripe | Snip | Blaze, extending to both nostrils | White face |

MUZZLE MARKINGS

| Snip and lip marks | White upper and lower lips | White muzzle |

The examiner may ask you:

- About any markings that are frequently seen on horses.

- To describe what a particular marking looks like.

- To identify a specific marking on a horse in the flesh.

PRT 2 EQUITATION

Everything covered in PRT 1

Each progressive test requires that the knowledge and practical ability accrued at the previous level be maintained. The aim of the progressive tests therefore is to build on each level, so that the earlier work is reinforced and consolidated. Remember to recap on the work you have covered at each level and keep the competence achieved; this will give you the foundation on which to build and develop greater experience and ability.

The examiner will look for:

- A sound level of ability appropriate to the requirements of PRT 1.

- Developing competence and confidence appropriate to the demands of PRT 2.

Be able to maintain a correct, balanced position at walk, trot and canter

As discussed in PRT 1, the rider's position is the foundation on which all future riding is built. Throughout your riding experience, a good basic position is always of major importance. As your riding experience continues, your suppleness, security and balance should all be improving. Work without stirrups helps this aspect of your riding, as does riding a variety of horses, because you must develop feel and balance for slight variations between horses' way of going. As you develop in confidence your enthusiasm for working without stirrups should improve as you begin to feel how this helps your depth of seat.

The examiner will look for:

- A basically secure and correct position (for PRT2) in all three basic gaits.

- Your ability to stay in balance without being dependent on the reins.

- A seat which is independent and a show of some overall suppleness and relaxation throughout your position.

Make turns and circles and know the aids for these movements

Within your riding lessons you should be familiar with riding basic school figures, turns, circles and changes of rein.

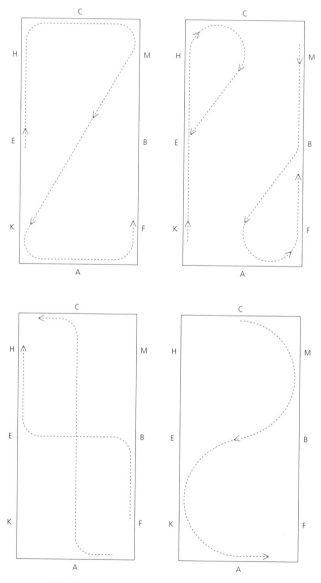

School figures: four methods of changing the rein.

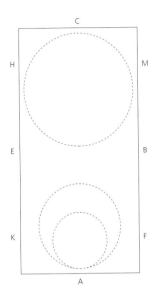

20m, 15m and 10m circles.

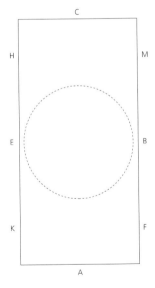

A 20m circle at B or E.

Your instructor should be constantly reiterating the aids that you use for any of these movements. The aids for turns and circles can be found in *The BHS Manual of Equitation*. Go through the aids with your instructor and think about them whenever you are riding and before you are required to ride a particular figure. Practise using the aids correctly when you ride, and also talk about them so that you feel familiar with describing them. Very simply:

- The inside leg creates energy 'on the girth'.

- The outside leg supports the energy, but also a little behind the girth controls the hindquarters and prevents them from swinging out, particularly on a turn or circle.

- The inside rein creates a little flexion in the head and neck primarily to follow the line of direction.

- The outside rein controls the speed of the pace and the amount of flexion which might be permitted through the neck.

The examiner will want to see:

- A rider who can influence the horse effectively, correctly and fluently to produce acceptable figures (turns and circles).

- A rider who can describe the aids that he or she is using for certain figures.

- A rider who has a basic understanding of how and when to apply the aids.

Changing the rein in rising trot and be able to change diagonal and understand the reasons for doing so

By this stage you should be familiar with the use of diagonals in rising trot. The use of diagonals, and changing of the diagonal as you change the rein, is to develop a supple, balanced horse on both reins. If only one diagonal is used, then the horse would build up muscles unevenly according to the diagonal on which you always chose to sit. This would not be in the interests of the horse's suppleness or ultimately in the rider's comfort. Changing the diagonal by sitting for one extra beat in the trot will facilitate your riding on the opposite diagonal.

Awareness of correct diagonals is something that develops with practice and feel. In the early stages it is wise and acceptable to 'look' to see which diagonal you are on. As your feel develops, you will gradually find that you instinctively 'know' when you are on the correct diagonal, and eventually you will be able to choose which diagonal you start to rise on. It does not matter in the least if you need to look. People vary greatly in the time it takes to develop 'feel' for the diagonal, and sometimes you will feel it more on one horse and not so much on another.

The examiner will want to see:

- That you maintain a good rhythm in rising trot throughout basic school movements (turns and circles).

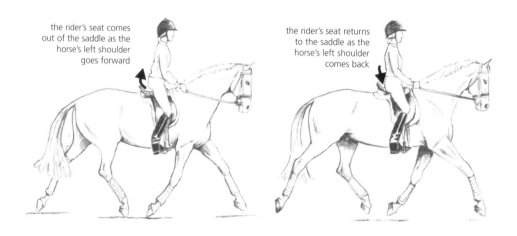

the rider's seat comes out of the saddle as the horse's left shoulder goes forward

the rider's seat returns to the saddle as the horse's left shoulder comes back

Rising on the correct (in this case, left) diagonal.

- That you show an understanding of which diagonal you should be on (sitting on the outside diagonal, i.e. when the outside front leg and inside hind leg are on the ground).

- That you can change the diagonal by sitting for one extra beat in the trot, maintaining a reasonable balance in rising trot before and after the diagonal change.

Work in sitting trot

Sitting trot, like the 'good basic position', is something that you will work to perfect throughout your riding life. Some horses are easier to 'sit' on than others. The secret of being able to sit comfortably to the trot is suppleness and relaxation in your basic position, allowing you to sit 'into' the horse not sit 'above' him. Work in your lessons to develop this suppleness and depth. Work without stirrups helps, as does changing from a few strides of rising trot to a few strides of sitting and then back again. Rather than thinking, 'I must take sitting trot' and tensing up in anticipation, think of sitting for just a few strides and then rise again. Feel confident about setting yourself a small, achievable goal. Gradually develop the length of time that you stay sitting. Consider how you make a transition to trot and you sit for the first few strides before rising. Concentrate on those first few strides and just stay sitting longer!

The examiner will look for:

- A reasonable ability to maintain a supple position which enables you to 'sit' to the trot.

- The ability to move from rising to sitting and sitting to rising trot without the horse showing a great disturbance of rhythm or fluency of gait.

- The ability to maintain basic good balance and independence of the rein in sitting and rising trot.

Walking over a set of ground poles

A 'set of ground poles' could be interpreted in a number of ways. Irrespective of how many poles we might be considering, the ultimate requirement is that you can 'steer' the horse/pony over the centre of the poles, making a straight line of approach and departure. For walking, the poles may be set quite widely apart and the requirement from the rider will be one of control of pace and direction to negotiate the poles.

In your class lessons you may well have started some work involving poles as a preparation for jumping. Jumping position is not referred to here, so as yet we will only consider the negotiation of the poles. In walk the rider's position needs little or no adaptation to walk over the poles. You feel the horse pick up his feet more decisively over the poles, and in this respect you should be ready to allow your hands to follow slightly more movement of the horse's neck forward as he steps over the poles. Your basic suppleness should allow your body position to follow any increase of movement that you feel as the horse steps over the poles.

It is probably wise to space yourself well away from another rider so that if a pole is dislodged, you are not so close that you follow over the misplaced pole before anyone can move in to adjust it.

The examiner will look for:

- Your ability to ride a good corner, straight line of approach and departure over the poles.

- Your ability to allow your hands to give the horse some freedom in his neck, to stretch a little as he steps over the poles.

- Your ability to maintain your balanced position as the horse steps over the poles.

Demonstrate work in canter on both reins and on the correct lead

Just as you will have learned about 'diagonals in trot' in your weekly lessons, similarly you should have been taught something about the 'leading leg in canter'. The horse canters in a 'three-time' pace, which means that when he canters, say, to the left, to balance himself he canters with his legs in the following sequence: outside hind leg starts the canter, followed by the inside hind leg moving with the outside hind leg, and lastly the inside foreleg – which we call the 'leading leg' – comes to the ground; then there is a brief moment of suspension when all four legs are off the ground at the same time. (Note: 'outside' is the right side and 'inside' is the left side when the horse is on the left rein. Simply remember that the inside always refers to the way in which the horse is bent, not to the direction of the school.)

You should be familiar with moving in and out of canter on both reins and understand the principle of the horse being on the correct leg in canter. Be clear that the balance of the horse is all important in achieving the correct leading leg in canter. Practise preparing yourself and the horse for making the transition to canter. Practise the 'feel' of the horse being on the correct lead so that you do not disturb your balance and position by looking down.

The examiner will look for:

- The way you prepare the horse to canter.

- How smoothly and clearly you apply the aids.

- The result of the horse being on the correct lead on both reins.

- Your ability to recognise if you have the incorrect lead and what you do to correct it. It is not a major problem if you have an incorrect lead in canter (as long as it is not produced by your poor balancing of the horse and aid application). What is important is how you deal with the fault when you recognise it.

Know how to carry and change hands with a short whip

A short whip will be up to 30ins (76cm) long. It has a fairly sturdy whip shaft, usually with a thicker thong/tab at the end of it. The easiest way to carry this whip is in one hand with the rein on the same side. The whip should be carried across the thigh, and the knob should be near the top of your hand. When you change the rein it is usual to change the whip, so that it is normally carried in the inside hand where it can support the rider's inside leg. When you change the rein concentrate primarily on the balance, rhythm and change of bend. Then, as soon as you can after a smooth change of rein, put the reins and whip into one hand, leaving one hand free. Take hold of the whip with the free hand, pull the whip smoothly through in front of your body, and retake the reins in both hands. The reins must always be taken into one hand or the horse will be subjected to a pull in the mouth as you swap the whip over.

The examiner will look for:

- A controlled, balanced carrying of the whip.

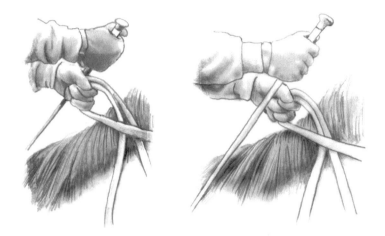

Changing a short whip from one hand to the other (as described in the text).

- The reins taken in one hand as the whip is transferred across.

- The whip carried across the thigh, with no tension or rigidity causing stiffness in the rider's hand.

Demonstrate how to adjust stirrups, reins, girth at halt and on the move

As a novice rider your stirrups and girth will have been adjusted and checked for you. Gradually you should take over this responsibility and build it into your standard procedure for mounting safely and making sure that stirrups and girths are safe and comfortable for you and the horse.

Reins should always be taken up and held at halt and on the move, even if the rein is relaxed and 'long' allowing the horse freedom to stretch.

You should learn to adjust the girth from the ground before mounting, then check it once you are on board, and again once you have ridden in for a few minutes. The horse will often 'blow himself out' when the girth is first taken up and then he will relax and the girth will be slack after a few minutes' work. Usually most safely adjusted from halt, make sure that the buckles are secure and the girth guard (if present) lies flat over the buckles.

With stirrups, become proficient at adjusting the length with your foot in the iron. Your instructor will show you this technique and then it takes practice.

Left: Tightening the girth while in the saddle. Above: detail of girth guard, a flap of leather which lies flat over the buckles of the girth.

Adjusting the stirrup length while in the saddle. Throughout, the rider keeps his/her feet in the irons for security.

If you eventually need to adjust your stirrups when on the move it will be much safer to do it this way, with your foot still in the iron, rather than letting the iron dangle free.

The examiner will look for:

- Your basic proficiency which demonstrates your practice of the task.

- That you are safe and competent at adjusting your own reins, girth and stirrups if no help is available.

Progressive Riding Test 3

STABLE MANAGEMENT

Demonstrate how to correctly apply a tail bandage

Using a tail bandage can be a regular task if you are involved in the care of horses that are used for competition purposes. These horses usually need their tails kept tidy by regular 'pulling' and then the daily use of a tail bandage. Tail bandages are often used for travelling horses to keep the tail from becoming rubbed in transit. You can read about the application of a tail bandage, but the

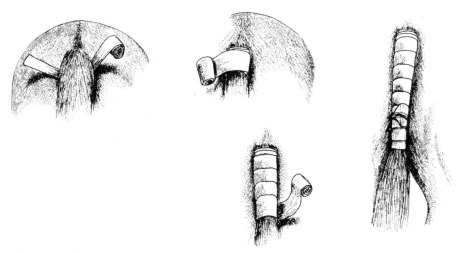

Putting on a tail bandage.

best way to learn exactly how to do the task is to watch someone competent put on and remove a tail bandage for you. Then you must practise the task regularly, first with someone supervising you, and then as often as you can alone. This will ensure that you are proficient at applying the bandage.

The examiner will expect:

- To see you handle the horse safely as you apply the bandage. (The horse must be tied up and he should not be too close to the wall as you apply the bandage.)

- To see you apply the bandage efficiently in a way that would enable it to stay in place and also do the job required of it.

Demonstrate how to correctly put on, take off and put away a rug and roller

The use of rugs for stabled horses is very commonplace and there are a huge variety of rugs available for every type of situation and weather condition. Rugs were traditionally held in place by a roller which fitted around the girth region. Nowadays rugs are more often held in place by cross-surcingles, which hold the rug on with crossed straps under the horse's belly. This arrangement alleviates the pressure which could be exerted by a roller around the girth. (Both rollers and surcingles are covered in this section.)

Putting on a rug is a task which you need to see done. Rugs are large and cumbersome, but they are easier to manage if you fold them in half before you put them on, particularly if rugging up a horse that is nervous, young or unfamiliar to you. Read about rugs, learn about the different types and their application, and then ask your instructor to show you how to place a folded rug over the withers, then unfold it into place and do up the front of the rug and the surcingles. It is then important to practise folding the rug and applying it yourself. Plenty of practice will make you competent.

Removal of the rug is another task which needs practice and correct demonstration initially. Always check that all straps have been undone before sliding the rug off over the horse's hindquarters and catching them before they fall on the floor. Rugs should then be folded and hung on a rack if they are in regular use; they can then air and stay fresh. If rugs are to be put away (e.g. at the end of a season) they must be stored in dry, moth-proof conditions and should

APPLYING A RUG.

Fold in half, place over the withers and do up the front strap. Unfold the rug over the hindquarters.

Attach the cross-surcingles.

always be put away clean and in good repair.

The examiner will look for:

- Safe handling of the horse while rugs are put on.

- Competent handling of the rug so that it does not disturb or frighten the horse.

- Competent and efficient fitting of the rug so that it will be comfortable for the horse to wear.

- All relevant straps adjusted to keep the rug in place, or, in the case of a roller, that it is fitted snugly around the girth just behind the withers with a pad to protect the back under the roller if necessary.

- Safe procedure during rug removal, including practical management of the rug.

- Practical treatment of the rug in storing it for future use, whether that be the next day or the next season.

Knowledge of various types of feed

In the yard where you ride it is probable that there are various different feeds used for different horses doing various different types of work. If this is the case, go and look in the feed room and see if you can identify what is there. A good stable management book will tell you much about feeding, which is a huge subject in its own right. Either attend a lecture about feeds (perhaps your yard will offer this), or ask your instructor to show you some different types. At this level, start to establish an interest in what horses might eat. If they are fed compound feeds or cubes (which many horses are these days) it is still useful to understand what components make up the manufactured feeds.

The examiner would probably expect you to:

- Know basic feed stuffs such as: oats, barley, bran, cubes, coarse mix, sugar beet, alfalfa.

- Recognise various feeds that are available and used in your riding school.

Know how to recognise different types of hay and whether the hay is good or poor quality

The two types of hay that you might be expected to know about at this level would be 'meadow hay' and 'seed hay'. In simple terms meadow hay is cut from permanent pasture or a field which is just shut up for a few months to grow on and make hay. Seed hay, however, is a specific crop of grass grown with the particular aim of providing a reasonably nutritious source of fibre ration to horses in work. Meadow hay is a softer, generally more palatable hay because of the wider variety of grasses in it. Seed hay would be regarded as a 'harder' hay and would be made up of only two or three similar types of grass which all come to seed at approximately the same time.

Assessing good or poor quality hay needs practice. Look at the hay in your riding school – hopefully it should be a 'good' sample. Good hay smells sweet or pleasant (not pungent); it should have a good colour and brightness to it. It should be free of dust or mould and should be flexible when you handle it (this demonstrates that it has a water content but has nevertheless been well made). Poor quality hay would be lacking in all these aspects. Ask your instructor to find some samples of poor quality hay for you to look at, handle and smell!

The examiner would ask you:

- What qualities you might recognise in good hay or poor quality hay.

- If available, you might have to identify good hay and bad hay and the difference between meadow and seed hay.

Know when to withhold water from a horse

Horses should usually have free and constant access to fresh, clean water at all times. The only exception to that rule which might apply to your level of knowledge is if the horse has worked hard and is hot and sweating. You should always cool down the horse gradually (making sure he does not catch cold) and not allow him to drink large amounts of water (particularly cold) suddenly if he is still warm and has not had water for a while. Water would then be allowed in small, regulated amounts every ten minutes or so, until the horse had completely recovered and was dry, warm and comfortable. Very occasionally water is withheld before medication is given, but this would be on veterinary advice. Immediately before strenuous exercise water would be regulated, but if the horse has had access to water at will then it is very unlikely that he will suddenly choose to drink too much just before competing.

The examiner would expect you to know:

- That water should be regulated to a horse that is hot and sweating immediately after exercise and that small, controlled amounts of water would be given gradually as the horse cooled down and recovered from the work.

Knowledge of whether a horse is healthy/unwell or ill

It is hoped that in the well-run riding school where you are learning to ride, the occasions when a horse will be ill are very limited. Thus this may be an area of knowledge where practical experience may be lacking. There are a large number of books on the market which will tell you, in very simple terms or in sufficient detail for a veterinary student, what an ill horse looks like and what might be the causes.

If we consider the definition of health then it is easy to consider when the horse is not well. Health means soundness of body (or mind). Ill means suffering from sickness or disease. Recognising ill health is very much a matter of common sense. If you know that a happy, healthy horse has bright eyes, an alert interest in what is going on, a shiny coat, appears to be eating, drinking and functioning well, and in general seems content with life, then recognising ill health would be the opposite of all these things. If you spend time at the riding school apart from when you ride, you will develop an awareness of what is 'normal' behaviour for horses, especially those you know. Just as with people, you begin to notice when things are wrong because you know an individual so well. Encourage your instructor to tell you if a particular horse is a little 'off colour' so that you can actually observe the differences from when the horse is well. If you have not been able to see a horse that is unwell then you must rely on learning the signs that would tell you that the horse was not feeling one hundred per cent. In PRT 1 you had to know the signs of good health; signs of ill health are largely the opposite of these.

The examiner will expect you to know:

- That the horse will be dull in his manner, not alert and interested with life in general.

- He may be off his food and/or water. He may be drinking more water than usual.

- He may have dull eyes and perhaps a discharge from his eyes and/or nose.

- He may look uncomfortable and demonstrate pain by pawing the ground, moving uneasily around and lying down and then getting up again.

- His coat may look 'stary', which means it is harsh and sticking up rather than sleek and glossy.

- His respiration may be quicker than normal.

Knowledge of different types of bedding available to the horse owner

Bedding is used for stabled horses/ponies and offers warmth, protection and comfort for the horse in the stable. Traditionally bedding falls into two categories. Absorbent bedding is any type of material which soaks up any wet or urine from the horse and therefore localises the fluid into patches of wet bedding. Shavings are a much used form of absorbent bedding. Drainage bedding is any type of material which allows the wet to pass through to drains within the stable floor, leaving the bedding on top relatively dry. Straw is a very common type of drainage bedding used for horses. Look around the yard where you ride and see what types of bedding are used. You already know about the basic management of a bed through mucking out, skipping out and setting fair, as this was required in PRT 1.

Some yards operate a system of 'deep litter', where the bed is not mucked out completely on a daily basis. Instead the droppings are removed and the bed is allowed to consolidate, with fresh bedding being placed on top of partly soiled bedding.

Find out which method is used in the riding school where you ride. Read up about both methods and discuss with your instructor why they use the method they do.

The examiner will want you to know:

- Several different types of bedding in every day use: e.g. wheat straw, shavings, hemp (Aubiose), shredded paper.

- That rubber matting is now often laid on the stable floor to reduce the amount of bedding that needs to be used on top.

Demonstrate how to fill, weigh and tie-up a haynet

Haynets are extensively used in many yards to offer horses a measured amount of hay (or haylage), which they can then eat with the minimum of waste from it being trodden underfoot. Many establishments use haynets to weigh the hay

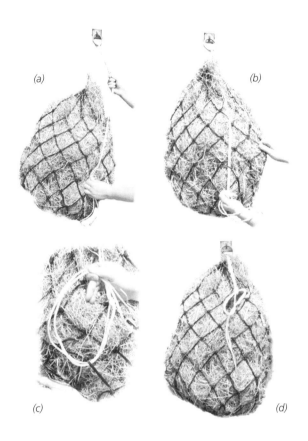

(a)

(b)

(c)

(d)

*TYING UP A HAYNET.
(a)–(b) Pull the net tight
against the ring. Pass the long
string through the net (c) as
near to the bottom of the net
as you can. Then (d) pull the
string well up the net and
secure with a slip knot.*

and then empty the hay onto the floor; this is done particularly at night so there is no risk of the horse being caught in the haynet during the night. Try taking a haynet and filing it with hay – it is not an easy task at first and you need to practise to become proficient. Open the neck of the haynet wide enough and then pack the hay into the net in manageable amounts. A haynet may weigh anything between 4lb (1.8kg) and 16lb (7.2kg). A 4lb (1.8kg) net would be an acceptable amount for a small early morning feed for a 16hh stabled horse in medium work, and 12–16lb (5.4–7.2kg) would be an appropriate amount for the evening feed (to last all night) for the same horse.

There should be a weighing device hanging up in the area where nets are filled so that the filled haynet can be hung on the spring balance weighing machine and measured. Once weighed you should be shown how to tie up a haynet correctly as there is a definite procedure for making sure that it is pulled high on the wall so that even when empty it will not cause the horse any inconvenience.

The examiner would look for:

- You being familiar with the handling of a haynet.

- The haynet being opened wide so that hay can be easily pushed into it.

- The drawstring on the net pulled up when enough hay is estimated.

- The net weighed and more added if it is too light.

- The haynet must always be tied up safely, as an empty haynet tied in such a way that it dangles limply in the stable around the horse's feet is extremely dangerous.

- A correctly tied haynet.

Know how to fit a saddle and snaffle bridle correctly

In PRT 1 you were required to know the parts of the saddle and snaffle bridle. By now you should be able to tack up a horse yourself. Learning to put on a saddle and bridle should always be done with demonstration at first, and then much help and guidance until you become confident about putting the tack in the right place so as not to disturb the horse.

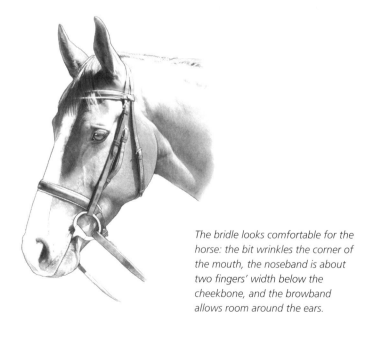

The bridle looks comfortable for the horse: the bit wrinkles the corner of the mouth, the noseband is about two fingers' width below the cheekbone, and the browband allows room around the ears.

At first you will put tack on a horse that you know and that perhaps you will be riding in your lesson. You will know that the tack belongs to that horse, i.e. it is his own saddle and bridle. The next stage is to understand and be able to fit almost any saddle and bridle. If you were confronted with a set of tack that did not belong to a certain horse, or if the tack for 'your' horse has been used on another horse and adjusted, you must be able to fit that tack so that it is safe and comfortable for the horse that is now going to wear it.

Taking the bridle first, ask your instructor to show you how to measure a bridle against the horse's head to see if it will be an approximate fit. Undo all the keepers on the straps so it is easier to adjust. If the bridle will go onto the horse's head without strangling him, or the bridle being so big that the bit is dangling out of the mouth, then put it on.

The examiner will expect you to know:

- How to fit the bit. (A snaffle should just wrinkle the corners of the mouth and not be too wide for the mouth.)

- That the brow band must not pinch the ears.

- That a standard cavesson noseband should be fitted two fingers below the cheek-bone and have two fingers' width over the nose.

- That the throatlash should be fairly slack so that a hand's width will fit in between it and the horse's cheek.

- That the bridle should look comfortable.

The saddle similarly:

- Must look appropriate for the horse.

- Must have between three and four fingers between the pommel and the wither.

- Must not pinch over the shoulders.

- Must have an even weight-bearing surface on either side of the spine.

- Must not be so long that it interferes with the loins.

PRT 3 EQUITATION

Everything covered in PRT 1 and 2

As previously mentioned, it is always possible that work already covered may be checked by an examiner when assessing your current work. All work with horses, whether in the riding or care, is cumulative. It is impossible to progress in knowledge and practical competence without always remembering, embracing and consolidating the basic principles.

Demonstrate an ability to ride forward

In the early stages of your riding it is demanding enough to think about maintaining your balance and position, to concentrate on when and how to apply the aids to communicate with your horse and to be able to think about basic school figures and transitions. Now you must also be able to influence your horse so that he is truly going forward. Some horses are naturally 'forward thinking', i.e. you need to use only very light leg aids to motivate them. Usually the beginner or novice rider will have ridden horses that tend to be less naturally forward thinking, as too much pace or feeling of energy can be disconcerting or even frightening. As your riding progresses you will ride a greater variety of horses, and it is then that you will begin to recognise the difference between a horse that easily travels forward with little assistance from the rider and the horse that you need to motivate and encourage to give you forward movement.

You must also learn the difference between speed and impulsion. Speed refers to the 'ground speed' or mph at which the horse is travelling, whereas impulsion is contained energy, or stored energy. Within your lessons you should be using frequent transitions, because these are one of the best ways for you to develop the 'feel' for when the horse is forward and 'in front of your leg' or behind the aids.

The examiner will look for:

- Your ability to maintain a basically correct position while being able to influence the horse through transitions into walk, trot and canter.

- Your ability to generate energy from your horse and then to be able to maintain him within a basic gait (walk, trot or canter) with a sustained rhythm and activity.

- To be able to show the tactful but effective use of a stronger leg aid or well-timed application of the short whip to support your leg aid and generate respect and obedience from the horse.

Make turns and circles and other school figures

Turns, circles and simple school figures should be fairly familiar to you, as you will have been riding them ever since you first joined a class lesson. While it is important that school figures are always ridden accurately, the quality of the way of going of the horse must be maintained throughout. In fact, it is more important to keep the horse going forward, with a good balance and rhythm than it is to ride a perfect-shaped circle but with the horse losing the pace. You will find that if you can ride the horse forward in a good rhythm and balance then the figures are actually easier to form accurately because the forward movement gives you far better ability to place the horse where you want him to go.

The examiner will look for:

- Your ability to ride accurate circles of 20 metres. You should be able to ride a 20m circle at A, C, E or B. It is easier to ride a circle at A or C where the three sides of the school will help you formulate where the circle goes. At E or B you will need a little more practice to ensure that you position the circle on the centre of the school.

- Turns across the school from E to B (and vice versa) or down the centre from A to C (and vice versa) would also be expected.

- A three-loop serpentine (see overleaf), with the loops being the full width of the arena, may be requested. This figure is ridden from A or C. This exercise demonstrates the rider's balance and co-ordination and also helps to maintain the horse's suppleness.

- Shallow loops on the long side (see overleaf). These are simple exercises and help to improve the rider's co-ordination and the horse's suppleness.

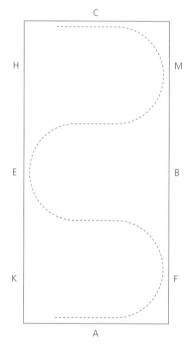

Three-loop serpentine.

Shallow loop (5m) down the long side.

- Half circles of 20m (from A to C or vice versa) or half 10m circles from E to B (or vice versa).

- Changes of rein across long diagonal lines, e.g. from M to K or H to F.

- If you are asked to ride any movement or figure which is unfamiliar to you then always ask for it to be explained before you attempt to ride it.

Describe the aids used to make turns and circles

For all the above figures the aids seem very similar when they are considered in general. That is largely because the leg and rein aids are applied as follows:

- Inside leg on the girth, to keep the horse forward and help the horse to bend by creating activity from the hind leg.

- Outside leg a little behind the girth, supporting the inside leg but also specifically controlling the hindquarters and preventing them from escaping outwards.

- Inside rein, asking for a little flexion in the direction of the movement.

- Outside rein, controlling the amount of bend through the horse's head and neck and regulating the speed of the pace.

Note: 'Inside' and 'outside' always apply to the direction in which the horse is bent, never to the inside or outside of the arena or school.

These aids can be applied in every instance of a basic turn, circle, loop or change of direction. The simple difference between the aid application for a circle and, for example, for a turn, is that for a turn the aids are applied for the duration of the turn and then released and the horse continues forward again, whereas for a circle the aids are applied and maintained until the circle is completed and then the horse is ridden straight again.

The examiner may ask:

- For you to describe the aids for a 20m circle to the left. In this case the inside leg and hand are the left hand and leg, the outside hand and leg are the right hand and leg.

- For you to describe the aids for a three-loop serpentine. In this case, for example, the movement might start on the left rein. The first loop would be inside leg (left) on the girth, outside leg (right) behind the girth, inside rein (left) asks direction and outside rein (right) controls pace and bend. Over the centre line as the bend is changed, so too are the aids. Inside now becomes right, as the horse is now bent to the right; outside now becomes left. Over the centre line the aids reverse again, as the horse is moved into the final left-handed loop.

Work over poles in walk and trot, showing balance and security

Work over poles may have been introduced into your riding lessons to add interest and variety (at the same time improving the work on the flat and your co-ordination of the aids) or as a preparation to jumping. If used for the latter you will have had the jumping position explained to you and you will have begun to practise it within your lessons if jumping is going to be the ultimate

Variations in the jumping position. A more forward position might be used for sustained work at a faster pace.

aim. The jumping position is designed to enable you to maintain a good feeling of balance and security over fences.

The examiner would be looking for:

- A correct position and a developing security, whether in your normal riding position or in jumping position.

- Your ability to ride a well-prepared turn towards a pole or several poles.

- Your ability to keep the horse on a straight line to the centre and at right angles to the pole(s).

Riding a straight line through the centre of, and at right angles to, the poles.

- Your ability to control the speed of the horse in the approach to the poles, to maintain a rhythm over the poles and then to keep an accurate line and consistent rhythm away from the poles.

- Your ability to maintain the above in both walk and trot.

Work without stirrups in walk and trot and perform simple supling exercises

Almost certainly your weekly lesson will involve regular work without stirrups. This develops the depth of your seat, your independence, suppleness and security, and gives you a secure foundation for taking your riding competence forward. Working without stirrups little and often is very beneficial and preferable to riding the occasional long stint – one long, hard session might make you tired and reluctant to work like that again. Supling exercises ridden without stirrups can be usefully performed on the move (usually in walk), and can also be helpful at a standstill (as long as someone holds the horse). Supling exercises improve co-ordination, flexibility and confidence in the saddle.

The examiner would look for:

- Reasonable confidence and balance without stirrups.

- Maintenance of the basic position without resorting to holding on with the reins.

- Flexibility and co-ordination in carrying out simple exercises on the move and at halt.

Be able to work in canter and describe the aids for canter

You should be confident in riding into and out of canter and understand the basic balance of the horse in canter. The knowledge of the correct aids and the timing for their application is important because you should know that the horse canters in a three-time pace. Details of the correct canter lead were discussed in PRT 2.

The examiner will look for:

- A more established ability to move into and out of canter smoothly, with good preparation and aid application.

- Your ability to describe the aids for canter: inside leg on the girth, for impulsion; outside leg behind the girth tells the horse to strike off into canter; inside rein maintains the bend; and outside rein controls the pace and degree of bend.

- Your ability to sustain the canter with some effect around the school on both reins.

Progressive Riding Test 4

STABLE MANAGEMENT

Know the importance of keeping stable tools, grooming kit, feed utensils and saddlery clean

In any well-run stable yard all these items should automatically be kept clean and in good order. If this is the case, then it may be very easy for you to take this for granted and not give any thought to the reasons behind it.

Each of these items can be regarded separately, but cleanliness itself should be considered part of good stable management. Cleanliness, generally, should be a reflection of a well-run, efficient establishment, and evident to any visitor to the yard.

Cleanliness of stable tools ensures a lower risk of infection brought about by harbouring dirt or germs.

Cleanliness of grooming kits ensures that the care of the horse's coat is carried out with clean equipment, which in turn will produce a more gleaming result. Clean grooming kit will also reduce any risk of skin disease brought about by dirty tools.

Cleanliness of feed utensils will be more pleasant for the horse and so reduce the likelihood of him refusing food. Illness could be induced by dirty feeding bowls.

There has been previous reference to the need for clean and well maintained saddlery. For the horse's comfort and well-being, and for the safety and comfort of the rider, clean tack is essential.

Look at the policy existing in your riding school for the cleanliness of all these aspects of good stable management. You should be able to trace regular care and cleaning sessions for all these items. For example:

- Tools might be washed and disinfected once a week.

- Grooming kits might be washed once a week.

- Feed utensils should be washed after every use.

- Saddlery should be cleaned after each use or at least once a week.

The examiner would ask questions on:

- The reasons keeping these items clean.

- What system you might adopt to ensure that cleanliness was maintained.

- What problems might arise if cleanliness was not enforced.

Knowledge of different saddles for different purposes

Go and look in the tack room of your riding establishment and see how many different types of saddle you can find.

You will almost certainly have learned to ride in a 'general-purpose' saddle, a design which allows you to learn to sit in a good basic position. Dressage and jumping, as specialist activities, dictate that you develop a more specific position, to enable you to perform that particular style of riding more effectively. The development of the 'specialist saddle' has produced designs which are appropriate to all disciplines: dressage, show jumping, cross country, showing, endurance, point to point, or racing. You may already have seen a dressage saddle (you may also have ridden on one) and perhaps some type of jumping saddle. Encourage your instructor to identify different saddles in your tack room so that you are familiar with the different shapes.

Generally speaking, a saddle which is designed for dressage is much straighter cut than a jumping saddle, which allows the rider to take a more forward 'jumping position' with shorter stirrups.

Consider the difference in the position you are developing in your work on the flat and how and why this differs from the position you adopt for jump preparation and jumping. You will then be able to recognise the difference in a

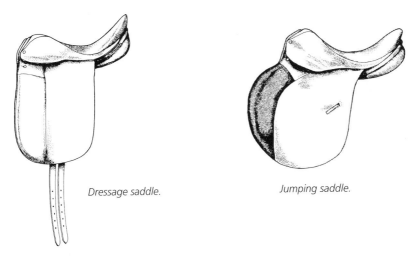

Dressage saddle.   *Jumping saddle.*

saddle when you first look at it. The more forward the knee roll, the more the saddle is designed for jumping. The straighter the panel of the saddle, the more likely the saddle is to be used for dressage or some other type of work on the flat, such as showing. A very forward-cut saddle which is much lighter than the saddles you may be familiar with, is probably used for racing. The saddles used in flat racing are extremely light and have no traditional 'tree' or substance because they need to be of minimal weight.

The examiner is likely to ask you:

- To identify a general-purpose saddle and a dressage saddle, and perhaps a jumping saddle, if there is one in your yard.

- To discuss why saddles are different for different purposes.

Different types of rug and how to fit them

If your riding school keeps a number of horses under different circumstances, e.g. school horses, livery horses for competition or training, and ponies at grass, then you will probably have seen a variety of different types of rug being used. This is always the best way to gain knowledge and experience. This practical observation can then be enhanced by further reading and study.

Depending on the time of the year, stabled horses are likely to wear a range of rugs which are designed for 'indoor' use, i.e. the rug will not be exposed to wind and rain. These rugs are usually made of synthetic material and are attached with a front buckle and cross-surcingles.

The rugs vary in thickness according to the weather conditions in which they will be used. Winter rugs are often heavily quilted for extra warmth, whereas summer clothing is more to keep flies and dust away, rather than to provide warmth. Some rugs are specifically for horses that are hot or sweating or likely to sweat, e.g. on a journey (anti-sweat sheet).

There is a wide range of rugs available for specific use when the horse is in the field. Whether the horse is turned out for an hour's leg stretch or whether he lives out permanently, there will be an appropriate turn-out rug for the circumstance. Most outdoor rugs are known as 'New Zealand' rugs. Their common properties are that they are waterproof, windproof and, in many cases, fairly rip-proof.

Take every opportunity to look at what a horse is wearing and if you are not able to work out why it might be in use, then ask your instructor to explain about the type of rug and its advantages and disadvantages.

The general criteria for a correctly fitting rug apply to any type of rug (see below).

The examiner would look for:

- Your knowledge of different types of rug and their names.

- When and why a specific rug might be chosen.

- How you handled the horse while putting on or taking off the rug.

- Your management of the rug. Some of them can be big and cumbersome. You need to learn to fold the rug into half so that it is easier to put on the horse – this avoids you having to 'throw' the rug over the horse.

- The rug should always be placed well forward and then slid back into place, allowing a little room for the rug to slip back naturally.

- The rug should fit around the neck so that it does not hang low around the front of the horse, and it gives enough freedom to move, but it does keep him warm around the neck and chest.

- The rug should be deep enough.

- The rug should be long enough to cover the horse's back.

Care of the horse after exercise

After your riding lesson you should be encouraged to be involved with the care of your horse and the procedure for removing his tack and making him comfortable. Whether the horse has been involved in an hour's class lesson, or whether he has just finished the cross-country course at Badminton Horse Trials, he needs care after exercise. The level of care will be appropriate to the intensity of the exercise that he has undertaken.

The examiner will expect you to understand:

- That the horse must be allowed to cool down gradually if he has worked so hard that it has made him sweat or 'blow'.

- That the horse should be walked around while he gets his breath back after exertion.

- That the horse should have a light rug or anti-sweat sheet put on to ensure that he doesn't catch cold from still being outside.

- That first the girth should be loosened and then the saddle removed if the horse has worked long or hard.

- That the horse is allowed water but in small amounts with intervals between, in case he has been without water for a long period – it is detrimental for him suddenly to have access to large amounts of water in such circumstances.

- That once the horse is comfortable he can have normal feed and water but he should be supervised regularly and into the evening to ensure that he is fine.

Recognise when the horse has risen clenches, overgrown feet, needs shoeing or has been recently shod

If you have never watched a farrier working (you may have seen one at your riding school) then there is much you can learn from him by observation. Watch the way he removes the shoe, ask him to show you where the clenches are and what it means when they 'rise'. Ask him to show you where the feet are

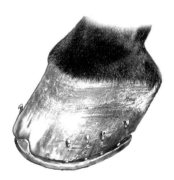

A foot in need of reshoeing: the clenches have risen, the shoe appears loose, the foot is long and in need of trimming, and the heel of the shoe is not supporting the horn.

A good, well-shod foot: the shoe fits snugly, the clenches are smooth on the hoof wall, and the heel of the shoe is long and supports the back of the foot.

overgrown and watch him trim off excess horn (much like cutting your finger nails when they get too long).

When you have read the section on shoeing in *The BHS Complete Manual of Stable Management*, go around the yard with the person who makes up the weekly (or fortnightly) list for the farrier. They should show you what risen clenches look like. Once the farrier has reshod a horse in the yard, look at the finished product; what signs can you see that tell you the horse has just been shod? Conversely what do you see when the horse needs shoeing?

The examiner will want you to know:

- What risen clenches look like. The nails, instead of lying flat on the wall of the hoof almost invisibly, begin to stick up above the surface of the hoof wall; the shoe loosens at this point.

- What an overgrown foot looks like. The toes begin to look long; when you pick up the foot, the horn appears to be growing beyond the outside edge of the shoe; the heels of the shoe may even look to be pressing into the foot.

- That a shoe(s) can sound loose, clanking on the concrete yard or on any other hard surface.

- That a shoe might be lost.

When a horse has recently been reshod, you should see that:

- The shoe fits the foot, and the foot is trimmed and tidily finished.

- All the clenches have been hammered flat onto the wall of the foot.

- The shoes are not worn in any particular areas specifically.

- The horse should move comfortably in his new shoes.

Rules for watering and feeding

Learning a list of rules is only a test of your good memory. If you take the trouble to ask why a rule exists, then the answers should enhance your knowledge and understanding of the subject.

We will consider the basic rules for feeding and watering with a brief explanation of each. Further study should be done in your own yard with your instructor; the information that he or she shares with you should conform to general principles for feeding and watering, and will relate to the individual horses and ponies in your centre.

The examiner will want you to know the following:

Rules for feeding

- Feed little and often. The horse has a small stomach in relation to his size therefore it is possible to overfeed him if you give him too much concentrate.

- Feed according to size (type and breeding) weight, type of work to be done, temperament and the level of rider who is to be coping with him. These criteria must be considered because if all horses of the same height were given the same amount and type of feed some would end up too fat/thin/lazy/sharp.

- Feed at least an hour before exercise, and longer for demanding work. The horse must not be trying to digest his food while being ridden – his system may direct blood to the muscles when in fact it should be going to digest his food.

- Feed good quality fodder. If poor quality food is used then the horse may well become ill, or just reject his food.

- Feed plenty of bulk. Horses were born to eat grass as one hundred per cent of their diet; to keep the digestion operating well the diet should include at least fifty per cent bulk intake.

- Make sure that fresh clean water is always available. The horse cannot live without water for more than a short period of time (days, rather than the weeks he would survive without food).

- Feed at regular times. The horse is a creature of habit; regular feeding times gives the horse a feeling of security and he will be healthier and happier as a result.

- Always feed in clean utensils. This is referred to earlier in this section.

With more specific reference to water:

- The horse should always have access to clean, fresh water. Water should rarely be withheld except under veterinary advice. Water might be regulated if the horse were hot or fatigued.

- Water should be changed regularly (minimum of twice a day) and observation should be made if the pattern of the horse's drinking changes (e.g. he drinks more or less).

Treatment of minor wounds

If you have spent some time in the stable yard where you ride, other than just having your riding lesson, you may already have seen horses with minor abrasions. Just like small children, horses can be quite accident prone, picking up small cuts and bumps from the everyday 'wear and tear' of living in a group (particularly with horses kept at grass). It is therefore essential that, as a person able to carry out basic stable management procedures, you learn about simple wound treatment. Take the time to read some publications on basic first aid for horses. *The BHS Veterinary Manual* is extremely comprehensive but would prove an invaluable investment from these early stages right through to advanced horse management. Wounds fall into four categories:

- clean cuts (incised wounds);
- lacerated or torn wounds;
- bruises or contused wounds; and
- puncture wounds.

Each type of wound has its own typical causes and the development of the wound is slightly different for each type. You would need to know that for all wounds the pointers listed below apply.

This is what the examiner would be looking for in your knowledge at this level:

- On finding a wound you should immediately inform whoever is in charge of the yard.

If needing to carry out first aid until a person of seniority arrives:

- If possible bring the horse into a stable or enclosed area for treatment.

- Apply cold water (from a trickling hose, if possible, or otherwise in cold-water swabs).

- Cold water will help to arrest bleeding and cleanse the wound.

- If profuse bleeding is apparent, apply direct pressure with as clean a piece of material as is available.

- Assist the member of staff who comes to take charge – he or she may require you to telephone the vet (the vet's phone number should be accessible to all, either in the office or veterinary cabinet in the yard).

- Understand that the priorities in any wound treatment are to:

  1. Arrest bleeding.

  2. Assess the damage.

  3. Call the vet if necessary, especially if there is any doubt as to anti-tetanus cover.

  4. Cleanse and dress the wound as appropriate.

  5. Monitor progress.

Knowledge of the daily routine of a yard that the candidate is used to working in

By now it is highly unlikely that you will have got this far with your progressive tests if you do not either:

1. Own your own horse.

2. Work as often as your time allows in the riding school where you take lessons.

You should be regularly spending part of a day or all day at the establishment, and in this way you develop the 'hands on' practical experience which can **NEVER** be learned from a book. Look at the daily routine of your establishment, it is bound to relate to the way in which that particular school operates. For example, if the school has a large number of ponies which live out at grass, then the day will allow a time for these to be brought in and prepared for work. If, on the other hand, the school horses all 'live in', then there will be no need for a time slot for bringing horses in from grass.

You must understand the reasons for having a daily routine and then be able to speak a little about the actual day in 'your yard' and why it is as it is.

The examiner will want you to know:

- Daily routines ensure that there is an organised system in the yard which enables everyone to know their role, what their responsibilities are, and roughly when they should be carrying out their tasks.

- Daily routines ensure that the horses are content and settled because they will always be fed at the same time (with exceptions for competition days, etc.) and will have a routine pattern of treatment.

- Horses are creatures of habit (as are humans) and everyone is more secure if routine is consistent.

- Routine ensures that nothing is forgotten and everyone is confident in their individual roles.

Explain the importance of a daily routine

This has been covered very comprehensively under the last heading; the examiner would probably ask you to:

- Describe the routine that you have in 'your yard' and why you think it is suitable for how that yard runs.

Know what a 'horse-sick' pasture looks like

You will, it is hoped, **NOT** see horse-sick pasture around the establishment where you ride. Well-managed pasture should never become 'horse-sick'.

If you look at small fields on the outskirts of big towns or cities, which are over-grazed and neglected, then you are likely to recognise 'horse sick' pasture.

The examiner would expect you to know that the following would be indicative of 'horse-sick' pasture.

- Too many horses or ponies on a relatively small patch of land.

- Many piles of droppings scattered around the pasture.

- Patches of smooth, well-grazed 'bowling green' areas of grass with few droppings interspersed by patches of lank, dark-green, long grass where the horses have fouled and will not eat the developing leggy grass.

- An abundance of nettles and docks and other hardy weeds (often ragwort) which deplete the grass and may be harmful to the horses.

- Often 'horse-sick' pasture may also have neglected or unsuitable fencing around it.

PRT 4 EQUITATION

Everything covered in PRT 1–3

These tests are 'building blocks'; the firm foundation from Test 1 upwards gives you the confidence and competence to build your expertise higher and higher. The foundation work must always be consolidated.

The examiner will look for a maintained level of competence from Test 3 and a developing skill at the next level.

Before mounting, check the saddlery on the horse that the candidate is riding, for correct fitting

Having completed PRT 3 Stable Management, you will have demonstrated

Incorrectly fitted bridle – bit too low, browband pinching the base of the ears, and noseband too high and pressing against the cheekbone.

Incorrectly fitted bridle – bit too high, browband pinching the base of the ears, and noseband too high and pressing against the cheekbone.

that you can fit a snaffle bridle and saddle correctly. You must now be able to look at a horse who already has his tack on and recognise that it fits correctly and comfortably. All the principles discussed in PRT 3 apply, but you must practise looking at horses as they come out to be ridden and ensure that their tack has been put on safely and correctly.

The examiner would expect you to be able to:

- See that the bridle is sitting comfortably on the horse's head – there should be no pinching around the browband, the noseband should not be pressing up against the cheekbone, and the bit should neither be pulling up in the mouth nor hanging too low.

- See that the saddle is not too low down on the wither, the girth is not pinching the elbow region, and the saddle doesn't look too big over the horse's loins.

Work over poles at walk and trot

This subject was discussed in PRT 3 and little needs to be added here. The only requirement is that the work should now be more secure and more established than at PRT 3. If jumping position had not been seen at PRT 3 then it would be a requirement here.

The examiner would look for:

- A degree of security in the jumping position.

- Straight lines of approach and departure.

- Control of the pace in approach and departure.

- Feel for rhythm over the poles.

Demonstrate work in canter on both reins recognising the correct lead and if necessary changing it

Your ability in working in canter must be developing through your basic weekly lessons. You should have an increasing awareness of when the horse is on the 'correct leading leg' and when he is on 'the wrong leg'. This must develop into 'feel' rather than a reliance on looking down, which will ultimately affect your balance and position and this will adversely affect the horse. As you develop this awareness you should also be practising bringing the horse smoothly back to trot if the lead is wrong and rebalancing the horse before giving the aid to canter again, so that he is able to answer the aid correctly. It is often tempting to 'throw' the horse back into canter with a hefty kick when he breaks, without 'reading' why he broke in the first place – because he was unbalanced and on the 'wrong leg'. He is in fact telling you something and you must learn to be a 'thinking, feeling rider'.

The examiner will look for our ability to:

- Ride well-prepared transitions to canter.

- Recognise when you are on the correct leading leg.

- Bring the horse back to trot when you recognise a 'wrong lead' and smoothly try to establish the correct lead.

- Deal with the situation constructively, rather than to 'punish' you for making the occasional mistake with a wrong lead.

Knowledge of horses' behaviour when ridden and in the field

This information can be found in many publications on stable management (*The BHS Complete Manual of Stable Management*) and other books on horse psychology. In your day-to-day handling of horses (or even if there is only weekly contact) you should be developing an awareness of how horses behave and what makes them 'tick'. This is perhaps one of the fascinations of contact with horses, learning to 'read' them – know what makes them content, happy, frightened or anxious.

The examiner would expect you to know that:

- Horses are herd animals; they live naturally in a group and are 'followers' rather than 'aggressors'.

- They gain confidence in a herd situation. There will be a hierarchy, or 'pecking order', when living in a field.

- In the field they run away from something which frightens them, they huddle together for warmth and to eliminate fly bother.

- They are browsers, relying on steady 'trickle' feeding.

- In the stable their ability to 'run' from the unknown is inhibited and they will therefore turn their bottom towards the perceived danger, hiding their head in the corner.

- If something alien is on their back they will buck, and if fearful of their mouth they may rear or bolt.

- When ridden they may 'spook' at things that frighten them.

Work without stirrups at walk and trot to perform some simple suppling exercises

This is to demonstrate your increasing independence of seat, and balance and co-ordination. Suppling exercises which you might be expected to perform could include arm circling to the rear, one at a time with the reins in one hand; and perhaps in walk, swinging the lower leg backwards and forwards to demonstrate looseness of the knees and relaxation of the lower leg.

Swinging the lower leg backwards and forwards to improve relaxation.

The examiner would look for:

- Balance and co-ordination in your position in walk and trot and through the changes of pace.

- The ability to perform the simple exercises without losing your basic balance or relying on support from the reins at any stage.

Progressive Riding Test 5

STABLE MANAGEMENT

Know a variety of feedstuffs and their respective values

At PRT 3 you were required to 'have knowledge of various types of feed' (see page 55). Following on from that knowledge it would now be appropriate that you understood a little more about the value that these feeds have in the horse's diet. It is not necessary at this level to have a lot of technical knowledge about feed values; it is sufficient to understand that feeds have an energy-giving effect on a horse, or may encourage him to put on weight, or may just keep him content. It would be a sensible progression from PRT 3 to discuss the respective values of the feeds we identified in that section, i.e. oats, barley, bran, cubes, coarse mix, sugar beet and alfalfa. There is a possibility that as Test 5 is the first test where you will be examined by someone other than the person who has been working through the tests with you, he or she might introduce a feed such as maize or linseed. Should this happen, try not to panic; try to have done some extra reading and research into feeds in general and always know a little more than the syllabus of any exam or test demands, then you will have that little extra in reserve when an unexpected question comes at you. Never feel defensive if there is a question to which you have no idea of the answer. If you genuinely have no knowledge of the subject, then say so. Never try to waffle about something when you have no knowledge. Always rely on the depth of your other answers to overrule one slight area of weakness.

The examiner would expect you to know that:

- **Oats** are regarded as energy-giving feed for horses in fairly hard work.

- **Barley** can be used for energy, particularly for a horse who is not good at keeping weight on. It tends to be regarded as a fattening feed so would not be good for an already overweight horse.

- **Bran** is often regarded as an old-fashioned feed and some people do not use it at all. It is valued for its fibrous properties: it helps horses chew their feed well; it may still be used as a laxative in the form of a bran mash. Care needs to be taken with feeding it because it is high in phosphorus and low in calcium and this can cause problems in the horse's system. (This last point is beyond the remit of knowledge of PRT 5 but would nevertheless often be taught and known at this level.)

- **Cubes** are manufactured, prepared feeds, moulded into cube shape. They contain all the nutrients required for good health and performance and are often designated for specific use, e.g. for brood mares, or (another type) for racehorses.

- **Mixes** are also manufactured feeds, but produced in a form where all the component grains are visible and the whole thing is bound together, usually in a lightly molassed form. Variations of mixes provide every requirement for the working horse in whatever capacity.

- **Sugar beet** is still widely used as a tasty, fibrous, economic feed for horses, providing a good source of fibre and calcium for the horse. Care must be taken with its preparation and management.

- **Alfalfa** is high-protein dried grass, cut when the grass is young and therefore high in nutrients and lower in fibre. It is a good source of calcium, and helps the horse chew his food.

Inspect horses for injury from ill-fitting tack and know how to treat these injuries

At PRT 4 you were able to identify poor-fitting tack and as a result of this you should be aware of the type of injuries that might arise from a poor fit. Relating back to wounds in Test 4, these injuries are unlikely to be large or traumatic, nor are they liable to produce profuse, if any, bleeding. They are more likely to be small areas of abrasion caused by continual pressure – rather like the injury we sustain on a heel when we have walked for too long in new or ill-fitting shoes. Such injuries may occur behind the ears, behind the elbows in the folds of skin around the girth region, or on the withers from downward pressure of the saddle.

The examiner would expect you to:

- Be able to identify the sites of these injuries.

- Be able to advise immediate cessation of work to prevent further damage.

- Treat the rubs with basic saline solution to cleanse them and then apply some proprietary brand of wound cream or powder to ensure infection is avoided.

- Review the fit of the tack.

- Prevent the horse from working again until the area has healed.

- Use a suitable girth, numnah, refitted saddle or bridle to prevent re-occurrence.

- Appreciate that all the above would be under the supervision of a member of staff in the yard.

Knowledge of how a group of horses or a single horse will behave in a field

Here again we are looking at horse behaviour, which was started in PRT 4. We have discussed how horses behave in the field when in a group.

It is very lonely for one horse to live permanently on his own in a field. Horses are gregarious animals and they have social needs fulfilled by living in a group, e.g. rubbing each other to scratch and comfort, running together for fun and exercise. Horses living alone are deprived of this social interaction, which in the author's opinion could be construed as a degree of cruelty. If horses are living together and one horse is left in the field while the others are removed, it is very likely that the horse remaining will become anxious. He may run around, and may even try to jump out to join his missing comrades. It is inadvisable to leave one horse alone in the field; either leave at least two or take all the horses out. If a horse lives on his own habitually then he may be used to living alone with no particular adverse signs visible.

The examiner would expect you to know:

- That horses in a field together generally behave as a group (see page 82 in PRT 4). The exception to that would be if one horse were ill and he may isolate himself from the main group.

- That horses are content when they are browsing, grazing or resting in groups, perhaps under trees or in a shelter. They may even lie in the sun if they feel secure and it is a warm, sunny day.

- That horses are stressed if they run about with heads up, nostrils flared, and huddle together at one end of the field looking at the perceived danger.

- Horses demonstrate a pecking order when fed in the field. Feed portions should therefore always be well spaced, with extra piles to accommodate movement.

- One horse should never be left alone in a field while the rest are removed.

Knowledge of the danger of taking horses out of their natural environment, what stable vices are and a description of the form each vice takes

We have touched on this subject when discussing leaving a horse alone and taking his friends away from him. This makes the horse anxious and insecure. Horses need routine and consistency if they are to feel secure. Horses are herd animals who naturally live in a group and graze at will. When we stable them we take them out of their natural environment and impose captivity on them for long periods of time, often 22–23 hours out of every 24. Stable vices can result. These are a range of repetitive habits, which the horse begins to demonstrate due to the boredom he feels by being confined. Some horses appear to be more inclined to develop stable vices than others, and there is increasing evidence of some of the habits having a hereditary predisposition. These considerations are beyond the remit of the knowledge required for PRT 5. We will name some of the commonest vices and give a brief resume of how the vice manifests itself.

This is the knowledge the examiner would want:

- **Weaving**: The horse stands at his stable door and swings from side to side with his neck. In bad cases it involves stress on the front limbs and is habitual. In mild cases it may only be seen in anticipation, e.g. at feed times.

- **Cribbing/crib-biting**: The horse grips the edge of his stable door or the window ledge and chews the wood or as a precursor to the next vice.

- **Windsucking**: The horse grips a ledge or door, arches his neck and sucks in air. In the long term this can cause digestive problems and even colic through the amount of air that is being dragged into the stomach.

- **Banging the door**: The horse kicks the door; this often starts as a bad habit in anticipation of feeding.

- **Box walking**: The horse never rests; he paces around his stable like a caged tiger, and often he always walks in the same direction, which is even more damaging.

- **Tearing rugs**: This is a destructive and expensive vice; the horse amuses himself by tearing his clothing off.

- **Kicking**: Some horses entertain themselves by listening to the sound of their own kicking – they stand at the back of the stable and repeatedly kick against the wall. In carrying on this vice they may injure themselves, to say nothing about the damage to the stable!

Be able to identify the farrier's tools

No doubt the farrier will visit your riding school on a regular basis. Take the time to watch him work. Observe the procedure for removing a shoe. What tools does he use and in what order? Ask him to identify the tools for you.

The examiner will expect you to know:

- **Buffer**: To knock up the clenches.

- **Driving hammer**: Used in conjunction with the buffer to knock up the clenches.

- **Pincers**: To prise the shoe off the foot.

- **Hoof cutters**: To trim excess horn.

- **Drawing or paring knife**: To trim the frog and tidy the foot.

FARRIER'S TOOLS

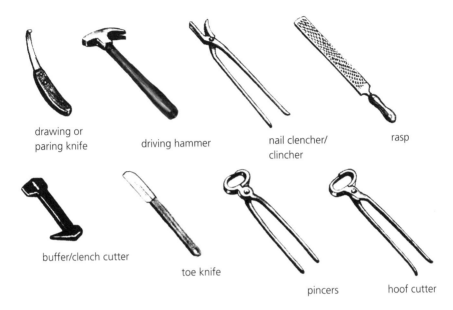

drawing or
paring knife

driving hammer

nail clencher/
clincher

rasp

buffer/clench cutter

toe knife

pincers

hoof cutter

- **Rasp**: To level the foot and finally tidy the foot after refitting the shoe.

- **Pritchel**: To carry a hot shoe.

- **Tripod**: To rest the foot on for trimming.

- **Anvil**: To prepare the shoe.

Knowledge of the aims of The British Horse Society

By studying for these Progressive Riding Tests, written specifically for people like you who are developing an enjoyment of the horse and his world, it is hoped that in due course you will embrace the aims of The British Horse Society and become a member (if you are not already a member).

The examiner would like you to know that:

- The BHS is the biggest membership organisation in Great Britain committed to the welfare of the horse in every aspect.

- It is the leading equestrian membership organisation catering for the leisure rider.

- It is the governing body for professional qualifications for those wishing to teach in the horse industry.

- It is a charity whose aims are to:

  1. Improve the standard of equine welfare throughout the country.

  2. Improve the standard of equitation and horse knowledge among all sectors of the riding public.

  3. Make riding a safer activity by encouraging the best standards of road safety and use of hi-viz gear.

  4. Improve access to off-road riding routes in the countryside and urban green spaces.

  5. Create awareness of the value of the horse through the media, to government and to the general public.

  6. Provide, regulate and monitor the Society's professional instructors' examinations.

  7. Provide benefits to members.

Know why horses should be regularly wormed

Horses, particularly those living at grass, suffer from varying degrees of infestation of internal parasites, commonly known as 'worms'. This is a subject that will be investigated in greater detail the higher you progress in your equestrian knowledge.

The examiner would expect you to know that:

- Horses suffer from internal parasite infestation (worms), which they pick up from ingesting larvae while grazing. The larvae migrate in the horse's system and can cause internal damage if not eradicated and allowed to multiply in large numbers.

- Regular worming may involve a variety of methods based on oral application of paste or powder, or introduction of a worm dose in the feed.

- Regularity of worming varies on veterinary advice and may be twice a year to every six to eight weeks.

- Types of wormer are very varied, as are the different species of worms that can infect horses.

PRT 5 EQUITATION

Everything covered in PRT 1–4

Keep developing the basic foundation of your riding skill with a more established and effective position. Practise the timing and co-ordination of your aids and work to develop a greater awareness and 'feel' for your horse. Test 5 will be the first test where you may be tested by someone who is not your regular teacher. It may be a senior instructor in the same establishment, or it may be someone who visits from outside. In both instances there is likely to be a slightly raised level of apprehension because you are no longer working within a familiar situation.

Run up a horse in hand

You should certainly be familiar with leading horses in hand. You will have done this on many occasions taking your horse to the school to ride. You may also have led horses in and out from the field. Running a horse up in hand is something that would be required of you if you were showing off a horse, perhaps for viewing for purchase, or for assessment of action, either by a vet or potential purchaser.

The examiner would look for:

- Your ability to walk and trot the horse actively forward on a straight line.

- Your ability to maintain a light contact on the rein but allow the horse freedom of his head so that his action is in no way 'supported' by your hand on the rein.

- A smooth turn, pushing the horse away from you through the turn.

- Your ability to maintain a fluent rhythm, both away from and returning to the person 'viewing' the horse.

- You staying ideally in the region of the horse's lower neck or shoulder; you should not appear to be 'dragging' the horse behind you.

Ride school figures in walk, trot and canter

This should be a natural progression of your class lesson riding skill. You may eventually aspire to riding a dressage test, whether in a riding school competition or in due course if you buy your own horse. A simple dressage test brings together a series of figures and movements in walk, trot and canter. Usually each movement on one rein is at some time reciprocated on the other rein. The difficulty of tying them all together is that you must be able to rebalance the horse if you lose rhythm and harmony before you ask for the next figure or change of pace.

The examiner would probably expect you to be able to ride some of the following figures in walk, trot or canter:

- 20m circles (walk, trot and canter).

- Shallow loops (walk and trot).

- 15m circles (walk and trot).

- Turns across the school and down the centre (walk and trot).

- Half circles returning to the track (walk and trot).

Work in open order showing transitions from walk to trot and from walk to halt

In your class lessons you should now be familiar with working in open order; if not, then you must practise this skill. You must be able to choose the area of the school that you ride in, keeping in a space away from other riders, and be able to use judgement to circle away from another rider before you are too close.

The examiner will look for:

- Your ability to regulate the pace and ride in a rhythm in the school independently, away from other riders.

- Your ability to choose the moment to make a transition to walk, keeping the walk active and forward.

- Your ability to prepare and ride forward into trot and to maintain a forward, rhythmical trot, maintaining a good position in the school in open order.

Work over ground poles at walk and trot and in a balanced jumping position

This requirement has now been included in Tests 3 and 4 and is here again in PRT 5. Each time the examiner will look for the same criteria (so refer back to page 65) but for a little more competence, balance and security than at the previous level.

Understand and be able to describe the aids for canter

In learning to recognise which canter lead you are on and whether the horse is on the correct or wrong lead, which you were required to do at PRT 4, it would be very unlikely that your instructor would not have already covered the aids for canter and why they are applied in the way they are. At PRT 2, and then at PRT 3, work on canter leads and the knowledge of the aids for canter were asked for on page 67, so do recap on the knowledge.

The examiner will expect you to be able to describe:

- Canter is a pace of three time, and the horse's legs move in the following sequence:

  1. Outside hind leg.

  2. Inside hind and outside fore together forming a diagonal pair.

  3. Inside fore (known as the leading leg).

Note: 'Outside' and 'inside' refer to the direction of the horse's bend.

- The aids for canter would be:

  - Inside leg on the girth maintaining impulsion and bend on the girth.

  - Inside rein creating a slight flexion in the direction of the movement.

  - Outside rein controlling the speed of the pace and the degree of bend.

  - Outside leg a little behind the girth to control the quarters and to give the executive aid to canter.

Know the risks and responsibilities involved when riding or leading on the public highways

By now you will almost certainly have enjoyed hacking out in the countryside, as well as riding in group or individual lessons in the school.

Hacking out gives you the opportunity to practise the skills you have learned in the school. There are, however, added responsibilities when you do ride out and you should have been made aware of these by your instructor before your first hack.

HAND SIGNALS

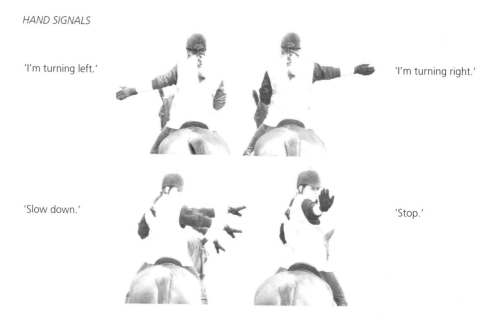

'I'm turning left.'

'I'm turning right.'

'Slow down.'

'Stop.'

Leading in hand on the road, staying aware and looking for possible traffic. In poor light, wear a fluorescent tabard.

The examiner would expect you to know:

■ That it is preferable to wear fluorescent clothing on yourself and/or your horse, giving high visibility to other road users, particularly in poor light.

■ (In the UK) The *Highway Code* as it pertains to horses.

■ That at all times you maintain a high awareness of what is happening around you.

■ The appropriate hand signals which may be necessary to use when riding on the road.

■ (In the UK) To stay close to the left-hand side of the road at all times (even when making a right-handed turn).

■ To ride in single file and only in double file when the road conditions and visibility permit it.

■ That if leading a horse on the highway, the horse must be wearing a bridle and the leader should position him/herself between the traffic and the horse, i.e. lead on the offside of the horse.

Progressive Riding Test 6

STABLE MANAGEMENT

Fit a New Zealand rug

A New Zealand rug refers to any type of rug which is used for horses going out to grass. The term refers to a waterproof type of rug, and there are many different types on the market. Some rugs are lightweight and shower-proof, for short periods of turn out, and others are much more heavy duty, with neck extensions and hoods providing overall protection to a horse living out in the field for longer periods.

The way in which these rugs are fitted and attached to the horse varies greatly from rug to rug, so make sure you know where the straps and buckles go before trying to apply a rug to the horse. New Zealand rugs fit in the same way as any other rug; they are just sometimes more bulky to handle and can be heavy and awkward when wet.

The examiner would expect you to:

- Check the rug and make sure that the leg straps are clipped up out of the way so as not to interfere when the rug is applied.

- Fold the rug in half, lay it across the wither and unfold it, rather than throw it over the horse.

- Fold the front forward and attach the front buckle.

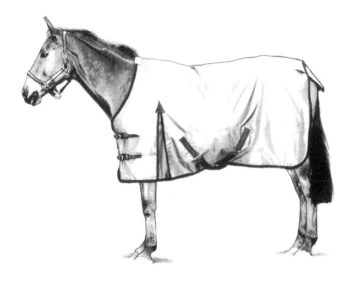

A well-fitted New Zealand rug, with gussets at the shoulder to allow for room and flexibility of movement.

- Fold the other half backwards and slide the rug into place so that there is still plenty of room around the neck.

- Attach any cross-surcingles or back leg straps.

- Check the overall fit and that all straps are safely adjusted and secure.

Understand the importance of water in a horse's diet

We all understand that horses (just like us) can live without food for several days, even weeks, but they can only survive without water for a very short time before the body begins to show signs of deficiency.

The examiner would expect you to know:

- Water aids digestion.

- It maintains the body temperature.

- It is a major constituent of blood.

- It aids excretion.

- It forms the basis for all the body cells and functions.

- It quenches the horse's thirst.

- It is a constituent of sweat, saliva and urine.

Make up feed rations for horses/ponies in light work (i.e. walk, trot or canter where the animal is not subjected to stress of any kind)

The best way to develop this knowledge and practical experience is to go into the feed room at your riding school and watch rations being prepared. Study the feed chart, which should be apparent on the wall, to see what each horse is fed. Ask questions about the types of feed that are used and why they are used. You then need to develop a basic understanding of how much a horse might eat in a twenty-four hour period, and, from this, appreciate that the ratio of bulk or fibre feed to concentrate feed must be appropriate to what work the horse does. If the horse is totally at grass his full intake will be fibrous (grass only, or perhaps supplemented with hay). If the horse is subjected to some work, he will need some concentrate feed to provide extra nutrients. In light work the ratio of bulk to concentrate is likely to be about 75% bulk to 25% concentrate. If a 16hh horse eats in the region of 12.5–13.5kg (28–30lb) of food per day then a ratio of 75% to 25% would mean that the ration would be about 9.5kg (21lb) bulk to about 3.25kg (7lb) concentrate. If 3.25kg (7lb) of concentrate was split into two feeds per day then the horse might have a 1.5kg (3lb) feed in the morning and a 1.75kg (4lb) feed in the evening; in between, the 9.5kg (21lb) of hay could be split up into at least three meals, with the largest amount fed at night to keep the horse going through the night.

The examiner would expect you to understand:

- The principle of working out the ratio of bulk to concentrate for a horse in light work.

- That having decided on the ratio and the numbers of feeds, how the fibre ration (e.g. hay) might be split up: for example – a.m. 1.75kg (4lb) hay; noon 1.75kg (4lb) hay/p.m. 5.5–6.3kg (12–14lb) hay overnight.

- That the feed ration may include cubes, or coarse mix, or some sugar beet, or alfalfa, all of which would be appropriate to horses in light work. That if two feeds per day are decided upon, then both feeds would have the same components, although one feed may be smaller than the other. (Again, give the largest feed at night.)

Knowledge of paddock management and basic maintenance

In PRT 4 we looked at the features of a 'horse-sick' pasture. The knowledge of basic paddock management will prevent this dire situation developing, whereby the pasture would need major management to rehabilitate it. In your riding establishment watch what work is done on the fields through the year; some activities will be seasonal and some will be ongoing. Discuss the paddock management with whoever is responsible for that area of the yard organisation. It is likely that you will find out all that the examiner would expect of you.

The examiner will want you to know that:

- Good paddock management depends on rotation of stock around the paddocks available, so that grass can have the opportunity to rest and recharge and is not constantly being grazed.

- The introduction of other stock (particularly cattle) helps to eradicate the worm burden specific to horses and also sweetens the pasture.

- Regular picking up of droppings from the pasture helps to keep the pasture as 'clean' as possible.

- Resting the ground after the winter if it has become heavily poached will allow the grass to recover.

- A policy of rolling and harrowing in the spring aerates the pasture and promotes new growth.

- Perhaps fertiliser could be used strategically, under advice, depending on how nutritious you want the grass to be (e.g. yes, for taking a hay crop, but no, if grazing fat ponies).

Know which plants are poisonous to horses

The examiner would expect you to know that the following plants are poisonous to horses:

- Ragwort.

- Deadly nightshade.

- Foxglove.

- Hemlock.

- Buttercup (large quantities).

- Acorn.

- Bracken.

POISONOUS PLANTS

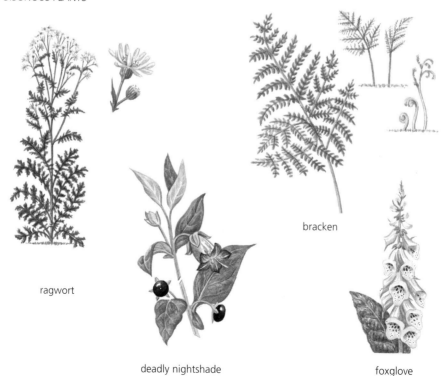

ragwort

deadly nightshade

bracken

foxglove

Know what to look for in and around a paddock on a daily basis

You may regularly go into fields to bring up ponies or horses to work. Do you make a mental check of the field when you go? Does anyone from your riding school regularly make a daily check of the paddocks where horses are turned out? It is easy to become casual about facilities that are used daily, until an incident or accident occurs, then vigilance is increased again.

The examiner would expect you to know that paddocks should be checked daily to see that:

- The fencing is in good order, with no gaps in hedges or rails displaced.

- There is no litter in the field which might be harmful to horses.

- There is no growth of poisonous plants.

- The water supply is clean and flowing.

- The shelter (man-made or trees/hedges) is in good order.

- The grass is healthy and sufficient (not too much or too little).

- The gate is in good order and secure.

Demonstrate the method for cooling off and caring for a hot horse after work

If you have ridden during the summer as well as the winter, you will almost certainly have seen a horse come in from work in a hot state. Learn from practical experience what is done with the horse and why. It is important that the horse is allowed to cool down gradually without the risk of catching cold or a chill, which could subsequently make him ill. Horses should always be cooled progressively, and the weather on the day will also have an influence. If the weather is hot and sunny, there is less risk of him catching cold than if he has worked up a sweat on a cold day and is allowed to stand around and catch cold without being cared for appropriately.

The examiner would expect you to be able to talk about and demonstrate the following:

- Walk the hot horse until he has stopped blowing hard and his respiration is nearing a normal rate.

- Loosen the girth but do not immediately remove the saddle, especially if he has been wearing it for a long time.

- Cover his quarters with a rug (especially over his loins which are vulnerable). If really cold, then put an anti-sweat type rug over his whole body.

- Once he has stopped blowing and if it is a warm day, you may wash him off with a hose, then remove the excess water with a sweat scraper and replace the anti-sweat sheet.

- If a cold day, you may decline from washing him and will instead rug him up with one or two layers, including an anti-sweat sheet, until he has dried off, and then you will brush him thoroughly to remove the sweat.

- Regulate his water intake while he is still hot – small amounts, frequently; do not allow him to gulp down a large draught of cold water.

- Monitor his recovery until he is one hundred per cent back to normal and comfortable.

PRT 6 EQUITATION

Everything covered in PRT 1–5

Completion of this section of PRT 6 will give you certification from 1 to 6, and if you so choose, you can use this as an exemption from taking the BHS Horse Knowledge and Riding Stage 1 examination. As with PRT 5, this test will probably be tested/assessed by someone other than the person who may have worked through the other tests with you.

The examiner will look for:

- A confirmed competence and confidence in all aspects of the previous PRTs.

Ride without stirrups at walk, trot and canter

Competence in riding without stirrups in all three paces is achieved in time and is part of your overall development as a rider. Early work without stirrups in walk and then trot is gradually developed to include canter.

The examiner will look for:

- Your ability to maintain a balanced position, independent of the reins in walk, trot and canter.

- Your ability to follow the movement of the horse in all three paces but particularly through the transitions in and out of the three paces.

- Some suppleness and lack of stiffness in a basically correct position.

Maintain a balanced, secure position at walk, trot and canter

This criterion is essentially linked to the previous requirement. It is necessary for the rider to be able to demonstrate a balanced, secure position with stirrups prior to exhibiting the same skill without stirrups.

The examiner will look for:

- The correct foundation of a good riding position in walk, trot and canter.

- The position maintained with confidence and some suppleness through the changes of pace.

Be seen to ride two different horses on the flat and/or over ground poles

If you have learned to ride in a riding school, it is very unlikely that you have ridden the same horse on each of your lessons. Demonstrating riding competence involves your ability to show the sustained skill on more than one horse. Try to ride a variety of horses in your lessons – some that require a more positive approach, if they are a bit on the lazy side, and some that are more naturally forward-going and may need a more tactful approach.

The examiner will want to see:

- That you can demonstrate an even level of competence, control and confidence on more than one horse on the flat and over ground poles.

- That you demonstrate an ability to adapt to a small degree if the horses you ride are very different in their way of going.

Work the horse as an individual

This follows on from the work in open order showing transitions, which you were required to demonstrate in PRT 5.

The examiner will look for:

- Your ability to control the horse independently while other riders are using the same area.

- Your ability to choose the work appropriate to how you feel the horse is going.

- Your ability to make transitions in and out of the paces in your own time and choosing your own space.

- Your ability to use the arena to maximum benefit for yourself and to stay out of other riders' space.

Ride a three-loop serpentine at trot

I would guess that this is already a very familiar school movement to you. You probably learned it early in your class lessons once you were riding independently. It teaches the rider co-ordination of the aids and the ability to feel the movement of the horse through several changes of bend.

The examiner will look for:

- Your ability to ride the serpentine in trot maintaining a fluent rhythmical trot.

- Your ability to position the serpentine so that the loops are of equal size and shape.

- Your ability to show a smooth change of bend through each loop, with you changing diagonal if you are in rising trot.

Demonstrate increase and decrease of pace at walk and trot

In simple terms this means that you can make the walk and trot slower and faster at your will. Later in your riding you will learn to shorten and lengthen the horse's stride, which means while maintaining the same energy you encourage the horse either to take shorter rounder higher steps, or you ask him to lengthen the stride and cover more ground with each stride. With shortening and lengthening, the speed or tempo should not change nor should the rhythm; all that changes is the amount of ground covered by each stride. Increase and decrease of pace simply means that you can make the horse go faster or slower in walk or trot.

The examiner will look for:

- Your ability to prepare the horse by creating more energy as you ask him to walk (or trot) faster (i.e. increase pace).

- Your ability to maintain the rhythm of the walk (four-time) or trot (two-time) as you ask the horse to increase or decrease the pace.

- Your ability to keep the horse active even when you are asking him to decrease pace (slow down) otherwise he will lose the rhythm of the pace.

Ride at walk on a long rein and a loose rein and understand the difference

Both these walks demonstrate relaxation. The walk on a long rein means that the horse may take as much rein from the rider as he chooses, stretching the neck out and down, while maintaining a fluent, elastic, ground-covering, marching walk. In a walk on a loose rein the contact on the rein is surrendered completely, and the only contact between the rider's hands and the horse's mouth is through the weight of the rein (which is held on the buckle end, completely slack).

Riding on a long rein.

Riding on a loose rein.

The examiner will probably ask you to show:

- A free walk on a long rein.

- A walk on a loose rein.

- You may be asked to describe the difference between the two walks.

Further Reading

The following books and booklets can all be obtained from the BHS Bookshop.

The BHS Complete Manual of Stable Management

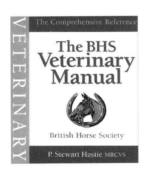

The BHS Veterinary Manual

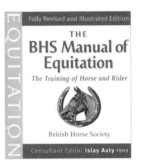

The BHS Manual of Equitation

The BHS Training Manual for Stage 1

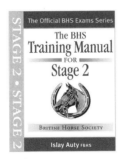

The BHS Training Manual for Stage 2 (in preparation)

The BHS Training Manual for Stage 3 and PTT

The BHS Riding and Road Safety Manual – Riding and Roadcraft

Guide to BHS
Examinations

Examinations
Handbook

BHS Guide to Careers
with Horses

Duty of Care

Useful Addresses

British Horse Society
Stoneleigh Deer Park
Kenilworth
Warwickshire
CV8 2XZ
tel: 08701 202244 or 01926 707700
fax: 01926 707800
website: www.bhs.org.uk
email: enquiry@bhs.org.uk

BHS Examinations Department
(address as above)
tel: 01926 707784
fax: 01926 707800
email: exams@bhs.org.uk

BHS Training Department
(address as above)
tel: 01926 707822
  01926 707821
email: training@bhs.org.uk

**BHS Riding Schools/Approvals
  Department**
(address as above)
tel: 01926 707795
fax: 01926 707796
email: Riding.Schools@bhs.org.uk

BHS Bookshop
(address as above)
tel: 08701 201918
  01926 707762
website: www.britishhorse.com

The BHS Examination System

Outline of progression route through BHS examinations

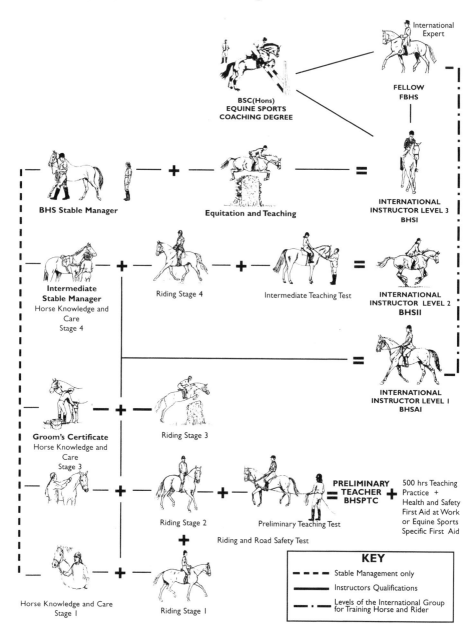

International Expert

BSC(Hons)
EQUINE SPORTS COACHING DEGREE

FELLOW
FBHS

BHS Stable Manager + **Equitation and Teaching** = **INTERNATIONAL INSTRUCTOR LEVEL 3 BHSI**

Intermediate Stable Manager
Horse Knowledge and Care Stage 4
+ Riding Stage 4 + Intermediate Teaching Test = **INTERNATIONAL INSTRUCTOR LEVEL 2 BHSII**

= **INTERNATIONAL INSTRUCTOR LEVEL 1 BHSAI**

Groom's Certificate
Horse Knowledge and Care Stage 3
+ Riding Stage 3

+ Riding Stage 2 + Preliminary Teaching Test = **PRELIMINARY TEACHER BHSPTC** + 500 hrs Teaching Practice + Health and Safety First Aid at Work or Equine Sports Specific First Aid

+ Riding and Road Safety Test

Horse Knowledge and Care Stage 1
+ Riding Stage 1

KEY

- - - - Stable Management only

———— Instructors Qualifications

—·—·— Levels of the International Group for Training Horse and Rider

notes

notes